THE NATIONAL ARCHIVES
AND
URBAN RESEARCH

NATIONAL ARCHIVES
CONFERENCES / VOLUME 6

Papers and Proceedings of the Conference on the
National Archives and Urban Research

SPONSORED BY THE NATIONAL ARCHIVES
AND RECORDS SERVICE

June 18–19, 1970
The National Archives Building / Washington, D.C.

THE
NATIONAL ARCHIVES
AND
URBAN RESEARCH

EDITED BY

Jerome Finster

OHIO UNIVERSITY PRESS

ATHENS, OHIO

Published by Ohio University Press for the
National Archives Trust Fund Board
National Archives and Records Service
General Services Administration
Washington, D. C.

Printed in the United States of America

Library of Congress Card Catalog No. LC 73-92905
ISBN 8214-0154-8

Contents

PANEL ON HOUSING

PANEL ON TRANSPORTATION

PANEL ON THE IMPACT OF
FEDERAL ACTIVITIES

Foreword

The National Archives and Records Service has inaugurated a series of conferences for the exchange of ideas and information between archivists and researchers. These conferences are designed to inform scholars about the wealth of useful research materials available in the National Archives and Records Service, as well as to provide an opportunity for researchers to suggest ways in which their use of these records could be facilitated.

The National Archives and Records Service, a part of the General Services Administration, administers the permanently valuable, noncurrent records of the federal government. These archival holdings date from the days of the Continental Congresses to the present.

Among the 900,000 cubic feet of records now constituting the National Archives of the United States are hallowed documents such as the Declaration of Independence, the Constitution, and the Bill of Rights. However, most of the archives, whether in the National Archives Building, the federal records centers, or the presidential libraries, are less dramatic. They are preserved because of their continuing practical utility for the ordinary processes of government, for the establishment and protection of individual rights, and for casting light on our nation's history when subjected to the scrutiny of the diligent scholar.

One goal of the National Archives staff is to explore and to make more widely known these historical records. It is hoped that these conferences will be a positive act in that direction. The papers of each conference will be published in the belief that this lively exchange of ideas and information should be preserved and made available in printed form.

ARTHUR F. SAMPSON
Administrator of General Services

Preface

The Conference on the National Archives and Urban Research held on June 18 and 19, 1970, was the sixth in the series of semiannual conferences sponsored by the National Archives. The choice of urban research as the broad subject for this conference derived from the convergence of several phenomena that made the calling of such a conference timely.

From the mid-1960s forward, a series of dramatic events in American cities engaged the attention not only of the public at large, but also that of governmental authorities at all levels and that of the academic world. The governmental response to these events has been a series of investigations and enactments and ad hoc commissions and more or less permanent agencies, the objectives of which have been discovery of the causes and the course of these events and the devising of ameliorative and reformative measures that should prevent such occurrences in the future.

The resultant federal concern with cities and their problems manifested itself in laws and executive and judicial actions whose application often involved direct contacts, on a scale only foreshadowed during the 1930s, with urban governments and, more notably, with other urban public, quasi-public, and private institutions. By the end of the 1960s some of the records of these federal activities had reached the National Archives or its adjunct organizations.

There was widespread agreement in governmental and academic circles that the urban outbreaks and the discontent that marked the 1960s were the culmination of long-festering social conditions, many of which dated from the remote American past. While federal researchers were concerned with recent data that might serve as the foundation for appropriate action, academics—principally sociologists, social psychologists, and historians—were interested in data of whatever period that might explain the evolution of present urban conditions. Some of these data, the staff of the National Archives knew, were to be found in federal records.

But apart from the interest in cities that arose in the 1960s, there has been an ever-growing preoccupation by historians and other social scientists with cities as a phenomenon in American life and with such factors that affected their development as the ethnic mix, housing, patterns of employment, residence, and transportation, and the distribution of wealth and power among their several constituent social groups. In increasing numbers there appeared books and articles about cities in general and specific cities and the methodology of urban research and history.

Historically, the initial heavy (on a national scale) involvement of the federal government with urban problems took place during the New Deal. By the end of the 1960s the passage of a generation permitted that era to be viewed in historical perspective. And such a view could well be heightened by examination of the documentation, now substantially complete, of New Deal agencies whose functions derived from and affected urban areas and their inhabitants.

The National Archives observed in the 1960s that a veritable parade of mature scholars, graduate students, and undergraduates visited its search rooms to use records of varied descriptions principally for their social data, not infrequently of nineteenth-century vintage, but also for their light on the federal impact on community life. With such evidence of an actual increased use of federal archives for urban research added to the other factors related above, it seemed an appropriate and propitious time to call a conference on the National Archives and urban research.

Mr. Jerome Finster, chief of the Industrial and Social Branch, who was chosen to direct the conference, has worked for many years with records of federal agencies operating in socioeconomic fields, particularly labor, transportation, and welfare. As an appraiser of records and, earlier, as a reference service specialist, he has come to know the potential of the records for urban research and the requirements of researchers.

The papers in this volume include those presented at the conference by the participating scholars (except in one case), members of the National Archives staff, and other federal officials. The volume also includes as an appendix a list of the National Archives staff papers that were prepared for and distributed at the conference. Taken together, these papers review the current state of specific aspects of urban research, the relevant data content of certain federal records now being generated, and several varieties of federal records in archival custody.

JAMES B. RHOADS
Archivist of the United States

Introduction

The general purposes of the Conference on the National Archives and Urban Research were to acquaint scholars with the resources of the federal government, and particularly the National Archives, that are useful for urban research (including historical studies) and to learn from them what should be done to better serve research in that field. It was believed that this exchange of knowledge would stimulate both the use of documentary sources previously untapped and the improvements of the collection and processing of relevant archives.

Although the holdings of the National Archives have primarily been used by historians, it was felt that the conference should involve representatives of other social sciences as well. Therefore, sociologists, political scientists, and scholars of other disciplines were invited to the conference along with historians, representatives of federal agencies whose work more or less directly affected urban areas, and selected members of the National Archives staff. In determining who should be invited as panel participants or guests, the conference director relied on his own knowledge of urban research and researchers and on the advice and suggestions of scholars experienced in or well acquainted with this field of study.

The invitation list reflected an effort to obtain mixes of scholars from various disciplines, various regions of the United States, and various age groups. The last represented a special effort to introduce the National Archives to younger scholars who had not previously attempted to exploit its resources. Also, recent notable contributions to urban research were taken into account in selecting guests and participants. It was particularly desirable to have on the program scholars among whose research products were some based on federal archival materials.

The working sessions of the conference consisted of four panels, each concerned with a broad subject. These four subjects were population, housing, transportation, and the impact of federal activities. Other subjects could have been chosen as well, but the first three of these were particularly reflective of the data in federal records relevant to urban studies, and the fourth subject was conceived as a context for providing a wide view of the problems and the documentation especially pertinent to the federal role in urban development.

The panel participants were representatives of the academic world, officials of federal agencies that were either concerned with urban development or collected urban data, and members of the National Archives staff. The academic panelists discussed some phase of research or the state of research in each of the broad subjects; the federal agencies' representatives spoke principally of their ongoing programs and data resources; and the National Archives staff members described bodies of records useful for urban studies.

Eleven National Archives staff papers were prepared for distribution at the conference and are listed in the appendix to this volume. Except in two cases, these papers describe bodies of archival records relating to specified cities that are illustrative of records for other cities. The two exceptions are overall descriptions of cartographic and audiovisual materials of urban relevance.

This volume contains, in order of presentation, the edited texts of the addresses by the archivist of the United States, the conference keynote speaker, the chairman of the Panel on the Urban Population, and (except in one case) the speakers on the four panels. Dr. Herbert Gutman, the speaker whose presentation is summarized but not reproduced, had a prior commitment to publish a work for which his conference paper is an integral part. Texts of discussions that followed the panels are for technical reasons not included in this volume.

The conference director is indeed grateful for the guidance he received from various scholars. Prof. Sam Bass Warner, Jr., of the University of Michigan, not only expressed an interest in the conference in its formative stages but also made valuable suggestions regarding speakers and persons who should be invited to attend and delivered the keynote address of the conference on its first day. Dr. Constance McL. Green, who on short notice assumed the chair of one panel, and Dr. Robert L. Zangrando of the Yale University Press both provided the names of scholars who could contribute to the conference.

The conference panels could not have functioned effectively without capable chairmen. For their assistance the director is grateful to Profs. Donald J. Bogue, Roy Lubove, and Benjamin Chinitz and to Dr. Constance McL. Green, who served, respectively, as chairmen of the Panels on the Urban Population, Housing, Transportation, and the Impact of Federal Activities.

The director must thank not only his colleagues who read papers at the panels and wrote the staff papers, but many others for their advice and encouragement. Katherine Murphy and Carol Morgan materially assisted in the preparation of the papers for publication. The combined efforts of many persons were largely responsible for the success of both the conference and, we hope, this volume.

JEROME FINSTER
Conference Director

THE NATIONAL ARCHIVES
AND
URBAN RESEARCH

Welcome

JAMES B. RHOADS

Archivist of the United States

I am pleased to welcome you to this Conference on the National Archives and Urban Research. Our conference director, Jerome Finster, has worked long and hard to arrange what promises to be a highly informative and useful program, and I am delighted that it has been possible for all of you to participate.

As you may know, this is the sixth in our series of semiannual conferences which began in 1967 with a conference on polar archives and which, since then, has included Conferences on the National Archives and Statistical Research, Captured German and Related Records, the Archives of United States Foreign Relations, and the History of the Territories.

The subject of each conference is closely related to records held in the National Archives, and each conference director is a staff member of the National Archives who has specialized in the conference subject.

A primary reason for holding these sessions is to provide opportunities for exchanges of historical information and points of view. We also want to focus attention on the research materials available in the National Archives. And, furthermore, we want to keep the dialog going between archivists and users of archives so that we can serve you better. Let us know your interests and your needs.

The subject chosen for this conference—urban research—seemed to us to be particularly appropriate at this time in history. There is concern everywhere about the critical problems of the cities. And, as always, man must look to the past for knowledge and guidance as he seeks solutions to urgent problems.

If this conference required a theme in addition to that of urban research, I think I would suggest the words of one of the tribunes in Shakespeare's play *Coriolanus*: "What is the city but the people?"

Talk though we do about population statistics and trends, about racial problems arising from overcrowding and discrimination, about the frustra-

3

tions of pollution-soiled and traffic-choked metropolitan areas, about the thousand and one problems of our cities, we are talking still about people and how they live: how they have lived in the past, how they live now, and how they will live in the future. Indeed, what *is* the city but the people?

I hope that in the two days of sessions beginning today new perspectives on America's urban scene will be opened by your discussions.

There have been some unavoidable changes in the conference program which I think I should mention at this time. After dinner tonight we had expected to hear from Daniel Patrick Moynihan, the distinguished counselor to the president. And he was to be introduced by the administrator of General Services, Robert L. Kunzig. Both Dr. Moynihan and Administrator Kunzig have asked me to express their sincere regrets to you. Each had to change his schedule and is out of the city. So, instead, we have arranged a special showing for you of two documentary films on the American city, and we believe you will find them of considerable interest.

In introducing the man who will keynote this conference I am reminded of Ralph Bunche's advice that "if you want to put an idea across, wrap it up in a man." This conference is concerned with a subject that has implications for the historian, the social scientist, and the archivist. Who, then, is better equipped to start it off than Sam Bass Warner, Jr.? Dr. Warner, of the University of Michigan's Department of History, is the representative of the Social Science Research Council on the Archives Advisory Council. He touches all the bases. Sam has contributed immeasurably to the effectiveness of the Archives Advisory Council, and he has been particularly helpful in advising us on many aspects of this conference.

The New Demand for Relevance
in American History

SAM BASS WARNER, JR.

First, I want to thank Jerome Finster, in behalf of everyone here, for his work this past year in setting up this conference. He has inquired widely and diligently throughout the profession to seek a representative body of urban specialists. Our panels reflect his careful consideration of the congruence between the Archives' holdings and some of the major categories of contemporary American urban research: population, housing, transportation, and the federal impact on urban development. I think he is to be congratulated for his expertise and thanked for the year's effort he has put into bringing us all together.

What I want to say this morning is that I think we are at the right place and that we are the right people who have assembled at the right time to begin important work. We are at the right place because we are at the place that contains the richest single collection of data to inform today's public agenda. We are the right people because we are a gathering of professional historians and urban social scientists; and the use of the archival material that provides the information the public needs is a good deal more complex than the more familiar library research. Finally, this is the right time because at this moment there is an impatient demand for research that will help people deal with today's society, and this is the sort of demand that urban social science can meet. In short, I regard our meeting as both propitious and urgent.

At the present moment the historical profession and the National Archives are, as they have been for many years, being actively pressed into canonizing the lives of the presidents and sustaining old national and regional myths. The elaborate publication projects devoted to the presidential papers of the saints (Jefferson, Washington, Adams, and so forth) and the lavish presidential libraries with their displays of relics, large parking lots, and tourist facilities, are part of the same spirit dedicated to the making of heroes for the public. The regional archives branches, as they expand, will doubtless

5

join this myth-making function, with each branch taking up the local genre: St. Louis, the westward movement; Atlanta, the Civil War; Chicago, the railroads and the immigrants; and so forth. I do not think it matters whether the impulse for this activity is professional, congressional, presidential, or popular culture; there is more important work to be done, and these tasks can better be left to the tourism of the National Park Service or a new entertainment division of the National Archives itself.

Today, there is once again, as there was in the Progressive period, a large, serious audience that wants useful history. I take the new demand for relevance in history, which can now be heard on every campus and at the professional meetings, to be a demand that as historians and social scientists we turn toward research, writing, teaching, collecting, and display, which will help today's people with today's problems. As Howard Zinn puts it in his excellent new book *The Politics of History* (Beacon, 1970), it is not necessary that everyone *turn to*, but there is a balance of subject matter to be redressed and a new audience to be satisfied. For myself, I think it is welcome news (and high time) that the present has become an open and legitimate focus for the examination of the past.

Such a concern for relevant history makes three kinds of demands upon historians. First, a political demand: historians must study the tactics whereby the goals of the society can be realized. Second, a subject matter demand: historians must concern themselves with the subjects of great urgency. Third, a technical demand: historians must devise methods to mine from the past the information that today's questions require, regardless of the forms in which the data were preserved in the past. I see no reason in our meetings over the next two days we cannot discuss all three kinds of demands in terms of the major panel topics.

First, the tactics. Given the national goal of creating a humane and inclusive society, how can such a goal be reached? What tactics might succeed when so many have failed? There never has been a nation like ours before; a nation with so much wealth, so far-reaching an imperialism, so large an urban hierarchy, so elaborate a government, so organized an economy. This uniqueness now reveals itself in the terrifying form of a racist, corporate, and military society that neglects the simplest needs of common life for the sports of science, business growth, and international dominance. Against this awful present, to guide us towards a different future, we have only the information of past experience and the hypotheses of social science. History, for all its failings, is all the data we have to help us understand what we now face. It is from the interpretation of historical data that we must make estimates about which tactics are likely to succeed, which are likely to fail. It is a grave responsibility and an enormous intellectual challenge for the historian to contribute information upon which he and others will take action to attempt to change their society. This role of analyzing the past to predict the consequences of public policy is by no means new; it has been played in recent years by historians attached to presidential commissions on crime, riots, and violence. Why can we not write with equal authority about poverty, health, education, housing, transportation, corporate regulation, and political control?

In the most general sense of public implementation of the goals of a humane and inclusive society, we have here in the National Archives the records of the ever-expanding efforts of the federal government. Here are the records of America's two experiments with full-scale socialism or state capitalism in the controlled economies of World Wars I and II. Here are the agency records of the ICC, the FCC, the HHFA, and many others, each telling of its failure to control its industry for the benefit of the general society, each unable to tame the local and regional political interests that swirled through and about it. Finally, in the records of the post–World War II era there is deposited the evidence of the beginnings of the military and industrial complex. As our contribution as professionals, why can we not begin to use these documents to provide answers to today's questions? For instance, what control of medicine and drugs would be likely to provide the public with cheap, safe medicine? And what tactics, given the past history of government failure, would be likely to achieve this end? What past housing projects and policies have proved successful? What were the politics of these projects, and what tactics would be most likely to make such projects attainable in the future?

I am aware that there are policy-studying organizations in Washington like the Brookings Institution or the Urban Institute that do just this sort of work; but these organizations have neither the time nor the staff for historical work. Moreover, as collections of a few scholars in Washington dealing exclusively with policy evaluation, they soon become captives of the administratively probable alternatives. They have neither the numbers, the time, nor the freedoms that independent historians can give to a reexamination of policy topics.

In short, if as historians we are willing to sign advertisements for the *New York Times* and if we are willing to troop to Washington to lobby with influential officials or to fill Pennsylvania Avenue and the Mall, then why can we not more profitably contribute our time in the very field in which we are expert, namely in the historical analysis of the urgent problems of our time?

Second, the subject matter demand. The current demand for relevance reaches beyond the immediate issue of providing reliable information for groups seeking effective tactics to achieve desirable goals. The demand requires a general shift in historical subject matter away from those issues that have become the accepted themes of our profession and out to all manner of topics that will provide a general background to modern life and modern institutions. Surely, the classic professional controversies over the Puritans, the Revolution, the Constitution, Jackson, the Civil War, Reconstruction, the farmers and the railroads, the bosses, and the Progressives can be attended to at a more leisurely pace. The very fact that we are a conference of urbanists shows where our priorities lie.

I would like to urge you all to be aggressive in this commitment. Our nation is urban, has been urban for some time, and is growing more so. Urban problems are now national problems, and there is hardly a national problem that does not manifest itself in our cities. What we must do is not to allow the growing popularity of our city topics to let us rest on our traditional subjects; but rather, we must move strongly out from our old ethnic and reform literature to meet the full range of subjects that city life contains. Cities are made up of banks, factories, electric utilities, small stores, auto dealers, unions, oil companies, hospitals, schools, churches, and so forth, and it is important that we write about cities this way. Since almost all these institutions and their related public issues were topics for federal programs in the twentieth century, the Archives contains the relevant data. Moreover, since the federal programs were national these records make intercity comparisons relatively easy.

Third, the technical demand. The demand for relevance imposes new technical burdens on the historian. It is frequently complained that college students, militant blacks, peace campaigners, and high school and community college teachers who are now demanding and experimenting with the new subject matter are antihistorical. It is complained that they proceed as if never before in our history had there been cities, class war, riots, government corruption, militarism, or elite greed. There may be behind this observable antihistorical behavior a strong ideological commitment, an attempt to free oneself from the constraints of the past; but I do not think that the trend is total. One very good reason today's subjects are often pursued without historical background is that the historical data are very hard to come by and their use requires a special effort and training that even most professional historians are unwilling to venture.

For instance, there are important historical contributions to be made to the following set of urgent questions. Why is the Chicago ghetto seemingly walled in by urban renewal and housing projects? Is there an employment policy for the young city dweller that will help him through school and give him a good start in the adult job market? Does the current form of our dispersed cities influence job access unfairly? What would be the consequences of a decent minimum income policy upon urban housing? Are public transit and rail transport saving the rich man's air at the poor man's expense? What are the active ingredients in white working-class racism? To what issues is the quality of municipal government salient? Can cities or states effectively control the location of industry?

The data wanted for these studies are not now in history books; indeed, they are probably not available in libraries. More and more, the basic social and economic data and background policy experience that we all need are in archives—in surveys and censuses and registration data taken by governments and their agents and in the records and the proceedings of governmental and private organizations. If it is a truism to note that since the Civil War the nation has been growing into an urban and corporate society, then we must note as well that corporate data are what we need. Corporations, public and private, issue reports, keep files, write letters; but by and large they do not write books. It is for this technical reason, among others, that I do not fear for our profession. It is here that the professional is necessary. Only historians and some especially motivated social scientists have the time, the training, and the imagination necessary to connect the fragments and the disparate sources of what will be, more and more, archival research necessary for the writing of the relevant history now so much in demand.

Thus it seems to be particularly fitting that we meet as a group of professional urban historians, men and women concerned with the essential subject matter of today, here in the National Archives which is the largest data bank of information that can tell us what we need to know if American history is to serve the vital needs that lie behind the call for relevance.

PANEL ON THE URBAN POPULATION

EDITOR'S NOTE

*The first speaker of the Panel on the Urban Population,
Prof. Herbert G. Gutman of the University of Rochester,
presented a paper entitled "The Negro Family in the
United States, 1850–1890." The editor regrets that, because
of Dr. Gutman's previous publication commitments, it
has not been possible to include the text of that paper in
this volume. Professor Gutman's thesis, however, is fully
presented in his book entitled* The Invisible Fact: A
Social History of the Black Family, *to be published in New
York by* Pantheon.*

*Using data derived largely from records in the National
Archives, Professor Gutman argues that the typical Negro
household in the United States before and after the Civil
War and Reconstruction was a two-parent family, that
Negro marriages in those eras were stable, and that neither
of these conditions was dependent on the occupational
level of the (male) head of the household. These findings
contradict the traditional picture, drawn by historians and
sociologists, of a matrifocal Negro family made more
unstable by its low economic state.*

*Because the remarks of Donald J. Bogue, chairman of
the Panel on Urban Population, contained substantive views
regarding the urban condition, they have been included
in this volume.*

Remarks

DONALD J. BOGUE

During recent months we have witnessed a great emotional catharsis over the American urban tragedy. We hear such dramatic terms as the *exploding American metropolis, population, hunger in the slums, failure of the older generation, the environmental crisis,* and so forth. I would like to submit that much of this is nothing more than confused oratory. It is designed to make headlines; to get a minute or two on the evening TV newscast; to stir up a following; or, perhaps, even to sell a book that one has written. I think that the time has arrived for a rebirth of urban research over the fundamental topics that are involved in this emotional upheaval concerning the metropolis. This research should deal with empirical fact in a historical perspective—an effort to establish principles and trends. I think that much of this crying of "tragedy!" is really nothing more than crying wolf. The truth of the matter is that a nearly ideal set of conditions for solving our environmental problems is now unfolding. I would like to cite for you ten happy hypotheses for the 1970s.

First, the polluted metropolises are *not* exploding. Most of them are growing very slowly, and the predictions are that many of them will actually lose population during the 1970s.

Second, the size of the elementary and high school population is now at maximum. It probably will remain the same or decline for the next fifteen years, yielding us an excellent opportunity to solve the so-called urban school crisis.

Third, the amount of absolute poverty, however we may care to define it, is declining—or at least it was declining until a recent upturn in unemployment—and is showing every indication of continuing this trend.

Fourth, Negroes are not outbreeding whites. The birth rates of the two races are rapidly approaching equality, and at the present moment, if one holds the differences in education constant, the differences are minuscule.

Fifth, juvenile delinquency is probably this year on the decline, and it will decline further in the future. There will be fewer juveniles "to be experienced" in the next ten years, and the ratio of adults to juveniles is rising.

13

Sixth, the Negro family is becoming more stable. It is not becoming more unstable, as was recently widely publicized.

Seventh, residential desegregation is on the increase. The suburbanization of Negroes is accelerating, and in the 1970s I think we can look forward to a great deal of desegregation, both of the socioeconomic and the racial variety.

Eighth, the overall quality of housing in the city is rising and will rise even more in the next decade.

Ninth, the quality of family life is improving. We are having fewer child marriages, fewer ill-considered marriages, and the overall quality of family life is on the upswing.

Tenth, the quality of the intellectual and social life in our cities is improving. As never before in our history, the grass roots man is informed about facts and issues. Instead of being disenfranchised rural sharecroppers, our poor are urban and are creative in the fields of music, art, drama, politics, economics, and education. Our national heritage is being enriched by the confrontation between the ghetto and the suburb.

I would like to end this listing by saying that we do have serious problems. They are not going to go away simply by themselves, but I think that they will be solved by careful research accompanied by well-planned and comprehensive programs, A well-aimed statistic is still a most powerful weapon for social progress.

Now, with respect to the international bias, I would like to end by saying that the relative poverty which underlies our domestic urban crisis gives us no reason to neglect absolute urban problems elsewhere in the world. The slums of Harlem, South Chicago, and Watts are places comparable to those of Lima, Lagos, and Djakarta. In Asia, Africa, and Latin America, we have obligations internationally which I think we cannot abandon simply because we want to give undivided attention and money to solving our urban crisis at home. Somehow we must work at both. I would not like to have as my neighbor an urbanologist who feels no sympathy for the plight of ghetto victims overseas. I do not think that we can afford to be the world's richest miser.

Growth of Urbanized Population in the United States: Past, Present, and Future

JEROME P. PICKARD

I do not want to come before this audience pretending to know very much about urbanization. As a matter of fact, as one deals with data and listens to people like Professor Gutman, or hears hypotheses like Dr. Bogue's, one realizes that maybe all the things we think are so, are not so, and most of the things we doubt are really true. However, I will take a partial exception to Dr. Bogue's first hypothesis on population explosion and cite staid old Boston as an example. If one considers not only the city of Boston, but also the seventeen surrounding cities and towns which form the core of the greater Boston metropolis, one finds that this core declined in population slightly by 3.4 percent between 1940 and 1960, while at the same time, the urban fringe of greater Boston, the remainder of its urbanized area, as defined by 1960 criteria, did explode. In staid old Boston, with its very slow growth rate and where the urban area went from only 2.1 million to 2.4 million over twenty years, the urban fringe nearly doubled in area and in population and stayed at the same density, about twenty-two hundred per square mile, over the twenty-year period. Now, I would submit that what we are talking about here is not an explosion in numbers of people but rather an explosion in space—what I call *decongestion*, or the thinning out of urbanization in terms of density at which people are living—and this type of change is one of the elements of the "explosion" phenomenon; and I think the word is rather unfortunate because an explosion, if it is a real one, does not leave anything in the middle of where it took place. Of course, that is not true of the so-called urban explosion; and (as I mentioned to him between sessions) Dr. Bogue has probably seen enough data on Latin American cities now to know that what we have is a fairly mild phenomenon by contrast.

I would like to quote from Prof. Louis Wirth of the University of Chicago:

> The degree to which the contemporary world may be said to be
> "urban" is not fully or accurately measured by the proportion of

15

the total population living in cities. The influences which cities exert upon the social life of man are greater than the ratio of the urban population would indicate, for the city is not only in ever-larger degrees the dwelling place and the workshop of modern man, but it is the initiating and controlling center of economic, political, and cultural life that has drawn the most remote parts of the world into its orbit and woven diverse areas, peoples, and activities into a cosmos.

Interestingly enough this observation was made in 1938 and published in the *American Journal of Sociology* in an article entitled "Urbanism as a Way of Life" (44, no. 1 [July 1938]: 2). I must admit that in my own work I have done little more than a doctor who takes a patient's temperature has done; that is, I have measured certain parameters or measurements of urbanization. And in preparing this paper and attempting to go a little deeper, I found that I clawed furiously and barely scratched the surface. This in itself, I think, bespeaks the great opportunity as well as the need for urban research. Urbanization is a multidimensional phenomenon, and therefore it needs to be discussed in a much broader frame of reference than simply population numbers or the spectacular growth of urban areas in their population and land coverage. I am going to discuss briefly four dimensional aspects: population and land, or the regionalization of urbanization; technology and stages of economic development; socioeconomic aspects of urbanization; and urbanization of the entire nation and its impact.

DIMENSIONS OF URBANIZATION

Population and Land

In the United States, unlike in Europe, urbanization has accompanied the nation's growth. In terms of people and land, urbanization has meant a continuous expansion in four dimensions: first, *a continuous increase in the number of urban places*, by whatever size measured; second, *a continuous increase in the individual population size* of the larger urban places (also reflected in a continuous progression of the urban population as a percentage of the United States total); third, *a continuing spread of urbanization* from its original nucleus on the Atlantic seaboard to the entire national territory; and, fourth, *continued decongestion of cities*, with new developments spreading out in the urban fringes at a fraction of the densities in the old city core areas.

Technology and Economic Development

In less than two hundred years the technological stage of transportation and communication has progressed from water transport, horse-drawn wagons, and pony express couriers to the modern age of high-speed air travel and instant communication by radio and television. Professor Borchert recognizes four stages,[1] but I have added a fifth representing the period since 1960. These stages are the:

(1) Sail-wagon epoch from 1790 to 1830;

(2) "Iron horse" epoch from 1830 to 1870 (the period during which the telegraph was invented);

(3) Steel rail epoch from 1870 to 1920 (the period during which the telephone was invented and became widespread);

(4) Automotive age from 1920 to 1960; and what I call (for lack of a better term) the

(5) High-speed communication—travel—amenity age, beginning about 1960.

Economic development has progressed from a dominantly agrarian society to a dominantly industrial-technological-urban society. The urban network has evolved from a series of very small towns and small city seaports in 1790, which functioned as trading centers in an agrarian society where four-fifths of the population were agriculturally employed, to the present national urban network that covers the country and has seen employment in agriculture diminish to 5 percent of the labor force.

Socioeconomic Aspects of Urbanization

Socioeconomic aspects of urbanization include progressively rising levels of education, income, access to communication (especially to rapid media, including newspapers, radio, and television) and a progressive spreading of urban life styles (and, I might add, technology) to larger and larger proportions of the American population, whether residing in urban areas or outside them. The last-named trend is not new; what is new is the degree to which the American population and the people in many other nations are becoming urbanized. American urban populations are heterogeneous in virtually all respects: physically, economically, socially, occupationally, educationally, and culturally.

The diffusion of both urban characteristics and urban-oriented population into the rural areas of the nation, especially those areas not far removed from major urban centers, has been very rapid in the last two decades. In

1. John R. Borchert, "American Metropolitan Evolution," *Geographical Review* 44, no. 3 (July 1967): 301–32.

a socioeconomic sense, urbanization of the population has less and less to do with relatively high population density, which is still the basis for measuring urban population, and it is becoming more and more a matter of individual life styles and modes of thought, type and levels of education, and daily economic and social activity.

In this evolution toward an urban nation, massive impacts have occurred in American life. In 1970, 42 percent of the nation's population is estimated to reside in forty-two large urbanized areas of more than 500,000 population each, and forty-two states are estimated to have an urban majority of their population at this point (I am predicting the 1970 census).[2] See tables 1 and 2.

The Supreme Court's one-man–one-vote rule for representation has emphasized the urban character of the nation. As of late 1967, for the Ninetieth Congress (thirty states had redistricted after 1963), 316 (or 73 percent) of the 435 representative districts had an urban majority of population.[3] In 209 districts (48 percent of all the representative districts in the Ninetieth Congress) the proportion of the 1960 urban population exceeded the United States average, ranging upward from 70 to 100 percent. Only 119 House seats represented districts with a rural majority, but these were distributed in thirty-nine states. Undoubtedly, the urban population impact will be even greater after the 1970 reapportionment.

Indeed, one wonders whether the urban-rural dichotomy is any longer decisive or meaningful in the traditional sense. The nation is urbanized, and "rural" areas are developing clearly complementary roles in serving an urban nation: providing living space for residences, recreation, water resources and food, minerals and raw materials, and a more open and less intensively occupied environment to counterbalance conditions in the crowded metropolises. With the mechanization of agriculture and extractive industries, rural producers now depend heavily upon the industrial products of modern urban society. With high-speed travel and the widespread use of motor vehicles, hordes of urbanites urbanize parts of the countryside on weekends and in holiday seasons, not to mention the millions of urban people who "live in the country" all or part of the year.

Urbanization of the United States Population

Table 3 shows the progress of urbanization in the United States from 1790 to 1940, as defined by two lower limits of place size. That table also dem-

2. At the 1960 census thirty-nine states had populations that were 50 percent or more urban. The final 1970 data did reveal that, in fact, three more states, Arkansas, Idaho, and Kentucky, had been added.

3. Eight additional states (including California and New York) redistricted in 1968; three other states which redistricted in the 1963–67 period made district changes in 1968.

onstrates the continuous growth in number of places and in aggregate urban population and the rise of the urban population from 5 percent to more than 56 percent of the total United States population.

The first reference to urban population cited by Truesdell was in the *Compendium of the Seventh Census, 1850:* "The census does not furnish material for separating the urban and rural population."[4] Curiously, exactly one century later, at the census of 1950, the Bureau of the Census finally perfected a method of identifying urban population in fringes around incorporated cities and their suburbs by defining "urbanized areas," as well as including unincorporated places of urban population size (2,500 or more population) in the urban population for the first time.

Previous efforts to separate urban and rural population on the basis of population size of places always tended to distort the urban population count by excluding urban fringes and by including some low-density areas. Philadelphia had a significant urban fringe in 1790, when the first census was taken; Boston developed one in the early nineteenth century. At the earliest census that defined and separated urban population (1880), the New York metropolis had already grown to a huge complex of 2.2 million population. It is almost unbelievable that we had a clustering of more than two million people in the largest urban area before urban population was ever defined in the census; looking back, I think it incredible.

GROWTH OF THE URBAN POPULATION

On the basis of the 1960 definition, the 1940 urban population of the United States (fifty-state area) was 78 million, or 59 percent of the nation's total. This expanded to 64 percent in 1950 and 70 percent in 1960, while total urban population went to 125 million—a growth of 47 million in two decades, for an annual growth rate of 2.4 percent! Even if all of the population increase in the 1960s went into urban areas,[5] as they will be defined in 1970, it would create a growth rate of something under 2 percent per year, so that the growth rate has slowed in the present decade, as has, of course, the national growth rate. Nearly 24 million of the growth between 1940 and 1960, or just over one-half of total urban growth, was added to the thirty-seven largest urbanized areas of 1960. Now that, I think, is highly significant: that half of all of the urban population growth in the twenty-year period was added to the growth of each of the thirty-seven largest urban

4. Leon E. Truesdell, *The Development of the Urban-Rural Classification in the United States: 1874 to 1949.* U.S. Department of Commerce, Bureau of the Census, Current Population Reports, Series P-23, no. 1 (Washington, D.C., August 1949), 16 pp.
5. All of it did; as revealed by the 1970 census; "rural" population in the United States remained virtually stationary at 54 million.

areas that as of 1960 which had a half million or more people (see tables 4 through 6 and the accompanying notes for further discussion of the growth of urban areas).

The trend toward concentration is found also if we look at the data on metropolitan areas. An extraordinary thing, when one looks at the history of these, is the stability of the group of the fifteen largest. In 1960 thirteen of the fifteen largest areas in 1910 were still among the fifteen largest; Washington, which was seventeenth in 1910, had moved up to the top group, while the only newcomer in 1960 among the top seventeen was Houston. A projection to the year 2000 suggests that there will be more newcomers in the South and the West added to the largest urban concentrations or metropolitan areas (see table 7 and accompanying text).

In the spread of metropolitanism, the urban region has now evolved. This has been described and defined by numerous authors. An *urban region* is a contiguous grouping of metropolitan and urban counties, a region of urban dominance with relatively high population density composed of a continuous series of urbanized areas and smaller urban places in close proximity and with a total population of at least one million. The archetype of urban regions, dubbed *Megalopolis* by Professor Gottmann,[6] is the largest United States urban region and extends along the Atlantic seaboard from southern Maine to northern Virginia, with a present population of about 43 million. This region was clearly emergent in 1900 when it extended from Philadelphia into southern New England. By 1920 it extended from Manchester, New Hampshire, to the Wilmington, Delaware, area. With the passage of time, urban regions become larger, but at the same time internal communication and high-speed access have been growing even faster; so that today, to get from one end of Megalopolis to the other is less of a journey than it was in 1900 when it was much smaller.

A projection of future urban regions, based on recent trends, indicates that more than three-fourths of United States population will concentrate in these regions by the year 2000, and in 1970 these future regions already contain 69 percent of United States population![7]

Spreading Urbanization by State

The many forces and influences which we call urban operate with higher intensity in the urban region. Most urban regions have a dominant regional

6. See, among others: Jean Gottmann, *Megalopolis: The Urbanized Northeastern Seaboard of the United States* (New York: Twentieth-Century Fund, 1961); Jerome P. Pickard, "Urban Regions of the United States," *Urban Land* 21, no. 4 (April 1962).

7. Subsequent research by the author in 1971, published in volume 5, *Research Papers*, Commission on Population Growth and the American Future, (Washington, D.C.: Government Printing Office, 1973), indicated a projection of twenty-eight ur-

center; a few have two or more. During the century from 1870 to 1970 the number of states with a majority of urban population increased from two to forty-two. Twenty-four of the fifty states are now involved in the development of a population metropolis of 1 million or more people; therefore, almost half of the states now have all or part of a large metropolis within their boundaries, although in about seven or eight states this is a fringe phenomenon (as it is in Kansas, for instance, where the Kansas City metropolis spills over into Kansas but by no means does the majority of Kansas population reside in large urbanized areas).

Urban Population Characteristics by States

Two characteristics, family income and adult education attainment, measure the relative socioeconomic level of the urban population. (See tables 8 through 14.) White and nonwhite groups are separated to eliminate major differences, although the inclusion of Spanish-American minorities among the white and of several distinctive ethnic groups (Orientals; American Indians) with the American Negroes, who constitute the great majority of nonwhites, tends to affect data in a few states.

Family incomes among urban groups in 1959 were distinctly lower in the South than in the rest of the nation. These differences were several times larger for nonwhite than for white urban population. Median educational attainment (years of school completed) for urban whites in 1960 was lower in the North than in the rest of the nation, probably because of the large population with foreign birth or parentage. Nonwhites, however, fared most poorly in the South and best in the West. Improvement in years of school completed is spotty, but was greater in the South for nonwhites than for whites; greatest in the North for whites; and significant for both groups in the West (see tables 12 and 14).

Urban Research Implications

A vast wealth of information about the United States urban population is available for analysis. Many studies have been made; however, a great majority of these are specialized types of inquiry. A potential exists for the analysis of the evolution of urbanization of the population in the United States; the spreading of characteristics and the changes in level of these; differences in urban population character derived from or induced by migration and the "absorption" of disadvantaged groups into middle and upper socioeconomic levels. Within individual metropolitan and urban areas is an

ban regions in the United States in the year 2000, with five-sixths of the nation's population concentrated in their total area of 503,000 square miles.

equally large opportunity for the time-series analysis of population change and movement; the evolution of so-called urban ghettoes of the poor; the growth and settlement of urban and suburban zones of distinct social and economic character; the rapid spreading of "economic urbanization" and of commuting beyond the physical boundaries of the urban mass. These are just a few items about which we certainly do not know as much as we ought to know.

A growing body of materials deals with aspects of metropolitan and urban evolution. Data-handling capabilities were never better. We can use more long-term analyses to improve our comprehension of the urbanization process. All these will provide significant new and improved information for shaping present and future urban policies.

TABLE 1. *Census Year State Population Reaches 50 Percent Urban*

State	Year	State	Year	State	Year
Ala.	1960	La.	1950	Ohio	1910
Alaska	1980[a]	Maine	1950	Okla.	1950
Ariz.	1950	Md.	1910	Oreg.	1930
Ark.	1970	Mass.	1870	Pa.	1900
Calif.	1900	Mich.	1920	R. I.	1880
Colo.	1910	Minn.	1940	S. C.	1980[a]
Conn.	1890	Miss.	1980[a]	S. Dak.	1980[a]
Del.	1920	Mo.	1930	Tenn.	1960
Fla.	1930	Mont.	1960	Texas	1950
Ga.	1960	Nebr.	1960	Utah	1930
Hawaii	1930	Nev.	1950	Vt.	[b]
Idaho	1970	N. H.	1910	Va.	1960
Ill.	1900	N. J.	1880	Wash.	1910
Ind.	1920	N. Mex.	1950	W. Va.	[b]
Iowa	1960	N. Y.	1870	Wis.	1930
Kans.	1950	N. C.	1980[a]	Wyo.	1960
Ky.	1970	N. Dak.	1980[a]		

NOTE: Five states reached the 50 percent urban population mark in the 1870 to 1890 decennial censuses; eleven states (including Hawaii, then a territory) in the 1900 to 1920 censuses; seven states in the 1930 and 1940 censuses; and sixteen states in the 1950 and 1960 censuses. Nine states are projected to reach 50 percent in the 1970 and 1980 censuses.

[a] Projected year.

[b] Year cannot be projected.

TABLE 2. *Mean Annual Urban Population Growth Rate, 1940–60*

State	Percent Per Annum	State	Percent Per Annum	State	Percent Per Annum
Ala.	3.4	Ky.	2.0[a]	N. Dak.	2.7[a]
Alaska	8.1[a]	La.	3.6	Ohio	2.1[a]
Ariz.	7.8[a]	Maine	0.9	Okla.	2.5
Ark.	2.7	Md.	3.1	Oreg.	3.4
Calif.	4.7	Mass.	0.9[a]	Pa.	0.9
Colo.	3.8[a]	Mich.	2.4	R. I.	0.7[a]
Conn.	1.8	Minn.	2.1[a]	S. C.	3.1
D. C.	0.7	Miss.	3.3	S. Dak.	2.7
Del.	2.9[a]	Mo.	1.7	Tenn.	2.6
Fla.	6.2[a]	Mont.	2.3[a]	Tex.	4.4
Ga.	3.3[a]	Nebr.	1.9[a]	Utah	3.8[a]
Hawaii	2.9[a]	Nev.	7.4[a]	Vt.	1.0
Idaho	3.0	N. H.	1.2[a]	Va.	3.9
Ill.	1.6[a]	N. J.	2.1[a]	Wash.	3.3
Ind.	2.1	N. Mex.	6.2	W. Va.	1.1
Iowa	1.4[a]	N. Y.	1.1[a]	Wis.	2.0[a]
Kans.	2.7[a]	N. C.	2.8	Wyo.	3.5

NOTE: The United States average for fifty states from 1940 to 1960 was 2.4 percent. An annual growth rate of 3.5 percent doubles the population in twenty years.

[a] Markedly higher growth rate in 1950–60 than in 1940–50.

TABLE 3.   Population in Places of 8,000 and Over and in Places of 2,500 and Over 1790–1940

Census Year	Total Population	Places of 8,000 Inhabitants or More			Places of 2,500 Inhabitants or More		
		Population	Number of Places	Percentage of Total Population	Population	Number of Places	Percentage of Total Population
1790	3,929,214	131,472	6	3.3	201,655	24	5.1
1800	5,308,483	210,873	6	4.0	322,371	33	6.1
1810	7,239,881	356,920	11	4.9	525,459	46	7.3
1820	9,638,453	475,135	13	4.9	693,255	61	7.2
1830	12,886,020	864,509	26	6.7	1,127,247	90	8.8
1840	17,069,453	1,453,994	44	8.5	1,845,055	131	10.8
1850	23,191,876	2,897,586	85	12.5	3,543,716	236	15.3
1860	31,443,321	5,072,256	141	16.1	6,216,518	392	19.8
1870	38,558,371	8,071,875	226	20.9	9,902,361	663	25.7
1880	50,155,783	11,365,698	285	22.7	14,129,735	939	28.2
1890	62,947,714	18,244,239	445	29.0	22,106,265	1,348	35.1
1900	75,994,575	25,018,335	547	32.9	30,159,921	1,737	39.7
1910	91,972,266	35,570,334	768	38.7	41,998,932	2,262	45.7
1920	105,710,620	46,307,640	924	43.8	54,157,973	2,722	51.2
1930	122,775,046	60,333,452	1,208	49.1	68,954,823	3,165	56.2
1940	131,669,275	64,896,083	1,323	49.3	74,423,702	3,464	56.5

SOURCE: Leon E. Truesdell, *The Development of the Urban-Rural Classification in the United States: 1874 to 1949*, U.S. Department of Commerce, Bureau of the Census, Current Population Reports, Series P-23, no. 1 (Washington, D.C., August 1949).

TABLE 4. *Growth in Number of Major United States Urbanized Areas, by Population Size Group 1800–2000*

	Number of Major Urbanized Areas by Population Size Group				Total Major Areas	Percentage of United States Population in Urbanized Areas	
Census Year	100,000–499,999	500,000–1 million	1 million–5 million	Over 5 million		Over 100,000	Over 1 million
1800	0	0	0	0	0	0	0
1820	2	0	0	0	2	2.5	0
1840	5	0	0	0	5	a	0
1860	7	1	1	0	9	a	3.5
1880	14	2	1	0	17	a	4.5
1900	30	3	4	0	37	33	12
1920	55	9	5	1	70	40	16
1940	79	9	9	1	98	51	23
1960	123	21	13	3	160	62	29
1980[b]	136	28	22	6[c]	192	70	41
2000[b]	151	29	35	8	223		53

SOURCE: Data for the period 1920–2000 was derived from *Dimensions of Metropolitanism* (Washington, D.C.: Urban Land Institute, 1967). Other data was compiled by the author from various sources.

[a] Data not available.

[b] Growth in number of areas after 1960 is slowed by mergers.

[c] Counting Delaware Valley (Philadelphia-Trenton-Wilmington).

TABLE 5. *Growth in Number and Population of United States Larger Urbanized Areas (500,000 Population and Over)*
1850–2000

	Number of Larger Urbanized Areas	Total Population (Millions)	Percentage of United States Population
1850	1	0.7	3
1860	2	1.6	5
1880	3	3.6	7
1900	7	11.0	15
1920	15	23.9	23
1940	19	36.6	28
1960[a]	37	65.9	37
1970[b]	42	85.0	42
1980	56	114.0	49
2000	72	183.0	60

[a] Alaska and Hawaii admitted as states in 1959 and are included in United States totals since that year.

[b] Data for 1970–2000 is projected.

TABLE 6. *Regional Location, United States Larger Urbanized Areas (500,000 Population and Over)*
1850–2000

Census Year	Total	Atlantic Seaboard[a]	Great Lakes[b]	California	North Central[c]	South	West[d]
1850	1	1	. . .	. . .	. . .	. . .	. . .
1860	2	2	. . .	. . .	. . .	. . .	. . .
1880	3	2	1	. . .	. . .	. . .	. . .
1900	7	4	2	. . .	1	. . .	. . .
1920	15	4	6	2	3	. . .	. . .
1940	19	6	6	2	4	1	. . .
1960	37	7	6	3	7	10	4
1970[e]	42[f]	8	8	4	7	11	4
1980	56	11	9	5	8	15	8
2000	72	12	13	6	9	21	11

NOTE: "Threshold" urbanized areas (a threshold urbanized area is the first in each region to reach a population of 500,000): Atlantic seaboard—New York-Brooklyn, by 1850; Great Lakes—Chicago, by 1880; North Central—Saint Louis, by 1900; California—San Francisco-Oakland, by 1910; South—New Orleans, by 1940; and West—Seattle, by 1950.

[a] Atlantic seaboard region, from Maine to Norfolk, Virginia, includes Albany-Schenectady-Troy, New York.

[b] Great Lakes region includes areas from Syracuse, New York, and Pittsburgh to Green Bay, Wisconsin, but excludes inland areas in Ohio and Indiana (Columbus, Cincinnati, Indianapolis).

[c] Exclusive of Great Lakes region centers.

[d] Exclusive of California; from 1960 forward includes Alaska and Hawaii.

[e] Data for 1970–2000 is projected.

[f] New larger urbanized areas added in the 1960s: Sacramento, Oklahoma City, Akron, Hartford-New Britain, and Rochester, New York.

TABLE 7. *Relative Rank of Leading Metropolitan or Urbanized Areas, by Population Size, 1910–2000*

Urban Area	1910	1920	1940	1960	2000
New York	1	1	1	1	1
Chicago	2	2	2	3	3
Philadelphia	3	3	3	4	6
Boston	4	4	6	7	12
Pittsburgh	5	6	7	10	21
Saint Louis	6	7	9	11	15
San Francisco-Oakland	7	9	8	6	5
Baltimore	8	11	11	12	17
Cleveland	9	8	10	9	9
Cincinnati	10	13	15	16	25
Minneapolis-St. Paul	11	12	12	13	20
Detroit	12	5	5	5	4
Buffalo	13	14	16	17	27
Los Angeles	14	10	4	2	2
Milwaukee	15	15	14	15	23
Providence	16	18	18	27	46
Washington	17	16	13	8	8
Houston	. . .	48	21	14	11
Miami	. . .	. . .	43	21	7[a]
Dallas	. . .	45	30	18	10[a]
San Diego	. . .	. . .	40	23	13
Connecticut City	. . .	. . .	. . .	. . .	14[b]

[a] In 2000, Miami extends to West Palm Beach, and Dallas merges with Forth Worth.

[b] Connecticut City does not exist as a total unit until the year 2000.

TABLE 8. *Index of 1959 Median Family Income of Urban White Families (1960)*
(U.S. Median = 100)

State	Index No.	State	Index No.	State	Index No.
Ala.	90	Ky.	87	N. Dak.	91
Alaska	135	La.	92	Ohio	103
Ariz.	93	Maine	83	Okla.	86
Ark.	77	Md.	110	Oreg.	98
Calif.	109	Mass.	98	Pa.	95
Colo.	97	Mich.	107	R. I.	88
Conn.	108	Minn.	101	S. C.	85
D. C.	120	Miss.	85	S. Dak.	87
Del.	111	Mo.	96	Tenn.	86
Fla.	84	Mont.	92	Tex.	88
Ga.	91	Nebr.	92	Utah	96
Hawaii	100	Nev.	114	Vt.	74
Idaho	91	N. H.	91	Va.	102
Ill.	112	N. J.	110	Wash.	104
Ind.	98	N. Mex.	95	W. Va.	90
Iowa	93	N. Y.	104	Wis.	102
Kans.	93	N. C.	87	Wyo.	99

NOTE: Median state was at index no. 95.

TABLE 9. *Index of 1959 Median Family Income of Urban Nonwhite Families*
(1960)
(U.S. Median = 100)

State	Index No.	State	Index No.	State	Index No.
Ala.	69[d]	Ky.	76	N. Dak.	e
Alaska	146[a]	La.	71[d]	Ohio	120
Ariz.	97	Maine[e]	e	Okla.	75
Ark.	55[d]	Md.	111[d]	Oreg.	122
Calif.	136	Mass.	118	Pa.	112
Colo.	124	Mich.	120[d]	R. I.	94
Conn.	122	Minn.	126	S. C.	59[d]
D. C.	129[d]	Miss.	57[d]	S. Dak.	e
Del.	103[d]	Mo.	98[d]	Tenn.	71[d]
Fla.	80	Mont.	e	Tex.	79[d]
Ga.	69[d]	Nebr.	112	Utah	131[a]
Hawaii	186[a]	Nev.	132	Vt.	e
Idaho	e	N. H.	e	Va.	88[d]
Ill.	125[d]	N. J.	125	Wash.	136
Ind.	118	N. Mex.	97[b]	W. Va.	80
Iowa	117	N. Y.	120	Wis.	131
Kans.	103	N. C.	70[d]	Wyo.	e

[a] Nonwhites of "other races" are more than 50 percent of the nonwhite population; Negroes are less than 50 percent.

[b] Nonwhites of "other races" are between one-third and one-half of nonwhite population; Negroes are between one-half and two-thirds.

[e] State has fewer than 1,000 urban nonwhite families.

[d] States in which nonwhite families were 10.0 percent or more of the total (1960).

TABLE 10. *Trend in Median Income of Urban Families, 1949–59*

State	Percentage of Change	State	Percentage of Change	State	Percentage of Change
Ala.	89	Ky.	79	N. Dak.	64
Alaska	a	La.	81	Ohio	80
Ariz.	92	Maine	80	Okla.	78
Ark.	82	Md.	90	Oreg.	72
Calif.	86	Mass.	85	Pa.	78
Colo.	85	Mich.	73	R. I.	78
Conn.	91	Minn.	79	S. C.	73
D. C.	58	Miss.	97	S. Dak.	67
Del.	94	Mo.	83	Tenn.	79
Fla.	84	Mont.	65	Tex.	73
Ga.	95	Nebr.	79	Utah	79
Hawaii	80	Nev.	86	Vt.	79
Idaho	73	N. H.	87	Va.	76
Ill.	79	N. J.	83	Wash.	75
Ind.	76	N. Mex.	89	W. Va.	75
Iowa	74	N. Y.	80	Wis.	78
Kans.	83	N. C.	72	Wyo.	63

NOTE: The United States median in 1949 was $3,431 and in 1959 $6,163. The change in the median was 79.6 percent; the change in the number of urban families was 25.4 percent.

[a] Data for Alaska not available.

TABLE 11. *Index of Educational Attainment of Urban White Population (1960)*
(U.S. Median [11.5 years] = 100)

State	Index No.	State	Index No.	State	Index No.
Ala.	101	Ky.	88	N. Dak.	104
Alaska	108	La.	101	Ohio	98
Ariz.	104	Maine	97	Okla.	103
Ark.	102	Md.	98	Oreg.	105
Calif.	105	Mass.	100	Pa.	93
Colo.	106	Mich.	97	R. I.	87
Conn.	95	Minn.	104	S. C.	101
D. C.	108	Miss.	106	S. Dak.	105
Del.	104	Mo.	93	Tenn.	97
Fla.	104	Mont.	105	Tex.	99
Ga.	102	Nebr.	105	Utah	107
Hawaii	109	Nev.	106	Vt.	100
Idaho	105	N. H.	92	Va.	105
Ill.	96	N. J.	94	Wash.	105
Ind.	97	N. Mex.	105	W. Va.	94
Iowa	104	N. Y.	94	Wis.	98
Kans.	105	N. C.	100	Wyo.	106

NOTE: Based on population 25 years of age and older and years of school completed.

TABLE 12. *Increase in Median School Years Completed, 1940–60,*
by Urban White Adult Population

State	Increase in Years	State	Increase in Years	State	Increase in Years
Ala.	1.3	Ky.	1.5	N. Dak.	1.5
		La.	2.6	Ohio	2.3
Ariz.	1.8	Maine	1.5	Okla.	1.5
Ark.	1.3	Md.	3.0	Oreg.	1.7
Calif.	1.4	Mass.	1.9	Pa.	2.4
Colo.	2.0	Mich.	2.7	R. I.	1.9
Conn.	2.6	Minn.	1.5	S. C.	0.3
D. C.	0.7	Miss.	0.5	S. Dak.	1.8
Del.	2.9	Mo.	2.0	Tenn.	1.7
Fla.	1.3	Mont.	1.9	Tex.	1.3
Ga.	1.7	Nebr.	1.7	Utah	1.3
		Nev.	1.4	Vt.	1.6
Idaho	1.5	N. H.	1.8	Va.	2.1
Ill.	2.2	N. J.	2.4	Wash.	1.6
Ind.	2.3	N. Mex.	2.4	W. Va.	2.0
Iowa	2.2	N. Y.	2.3	Wis.	2.4
Kans.	2.4	N. C.	1.2	Wyo.	1.7

NOTE: The United States median in 1940 was 9.1 years and in 1960 11.5 years, yielding an increase in the United States median from 1940 to 1960 of 2.4 years.

TABLE 13. *Index of Educational Attainment of Urban Nonwhite Population*
(1960)
(U.S. Median [8.7 years] = 100)

State	Index No.	State	Index No.	State	Index No.
Ala.	84	Ky.	97	N. Dak.	*
Alaska	113	La.	78	Ohio	105
Ariz.	99	Maine	133	Okla.	105
Ark.	83	Md.	97	Oreg.	114
Calif.	123	Mass.	118	Pa.	103
Colo.	129	Mich.	105	R. I.	109
Conn.	105	Minn.	123	S. C.	78
D. C.	113	Miss.	80	S. Dak.	111
Del.	100	Mo.	101	Tenn.	91
Fla.	85	Mont.	105	Tex.	98
Ga.	78	Nebr.	113	Utah	137
Hawaii	124	Nev.	101	Vt.	a
Idaho	126	N. H.	a	Va.	91
Ill.	105	N. J.	102	Wash.	124
Ind.	103	N. Mex.	107	W. Va.	101
Iowa	110	N. Y.	108	Wis.	106
Kans.	111	N. C.	87	Wyo.	114

NOTE: Based on population 25 years of age and older and years of school completed.
a Fewer than 1,000 urban nonwhite population.

TABLE 14. *Increase in Median School Years Completed, 1940–60,*
by Urban Nonwhite Adult Population

State		State		State	
Ala.	1.7	Ky.	1.7	N. Dak.	a
Ariz.	1.3	La.	1.6	Ohio	1.7
Ark.	0.9	Maine	a	Okla.	1.4
Calif.	2.3	Md.	2.3	Oreg.	1.6
Colo.	2.7	Mass.	2.2	Pa.	1.9
Conn.	1.6	Mich.	1.5	R. I.	1.9
D. C.	2.2	Minn.	2.3	S. C.	2.0
Del.	2.1	Miss.	1.2	S. Dak.	a
Fla.	1.6	Mo.	1.4	Tenn.	1.7
Ga.	1.7	Mont.	1.5	Tex.	1.7
Idaho	a	Nebr.	1.8	Utah	3.7
Ill.	1.4	Nev.	a	Vt.	a
Ind.	1.4	N. H.	a	Va.	2.0
Iowa	1.6	N. J.	1.7	Wash.	2.2
Kans.	1.7	N. Mex.	1.7	W. Va.	1.4
		N. Y.	1.7	Wis.	1.6
		N. C.	1.8	Wyo.	a

NOTE: The United States median in 1940 was 6.8 years and in 1960 8.7 years, making the increase in the United States median from 1940 to 1960 1.9 years.
a Nonwhite adult population smaller than 1,000 in 1940.

A General View of Urban Population Research Possibilities in the National Archives

WILLIAM E. LIND

In 1899 a book was published entitled *The Growth of Cities in the Nineteenth Century* by Adna Ferrin Weber. The book was the outgrowth of a statistical investigation of the growth of cities in the Western world in the nineteenth century, which the author had undertaken as research for a doctoral dissertation. In 1963 this work was republished by the Cornell University Press as part of a series of Cornell reprints in urban studies. This book has been described as the "first really sound comprehensive and complete contribution to urban studies by an American." Lewis Mumford has described this study as a "classic pioneer work." Up to the time of the original publication in 1899, the only comparable studies had been in French and German. The author was appointed by Gov. Theodore Roosevelt of New York to the post of deputy commissioner of labor statistics in 1899. Weber later held a post in the Census Bureau and was also instrumental in introducing workmen's compensation in the United States.

Of interest to the archivist and historian are Weber's sources and the uses he makes of them. As previously stated, Weber's work was a statistical investigation in which he drew certain conclusions and made certain generalizations concerning patterns of urbanization. Weber discusses such things as migrations from rural areas to cities, growth in size of particular cities, as well as social, ethnic, and economic factors. Weber also counsels planning for future urban growth, stringent health regulations, rent control, adequate transportation, public welfare, and other suggestions, all of which were regarded as visionary at the time. The source material used as far as American cities are concerned relied mainly on the compendium of the eleventh census of the United States, which in turn was compiled from the original census records of that year. Weber's work is remarkable because he did not have the advantages of the urban researcher of today. For American cities he had to confine himself mainly to the findings of the Bureau of the Census as far as federal records were concerned. The question is, were there other government records at this time which would have been of use to him? Our federal

31

government, which was not as socially oriented as it is today, must have had material that would have been useful to the urban researcher. But how could Weber know, or if he knew, have access to such materials? The National Archives was still thirty-five years away. Also, Leland's and Van Tyne's famous guide was still several years away.

Today the urban researcher has the resources of the National Archives. Not only does this researcher have the advantage of the physical and record facilities of the National Archives, he also has through the expertise of its staff members liaison with other federal sources to aid him in his research. Today I will attempt to briefly suggest some sources of urban research in the National Archives in terms of past, present, and future. By past I mean records in our custody for the nineteenth century up to World War I. These are records which the then new school of "scientific method" historians could have used at the turn of the century had they been available. Records of the present are those records from World War I to the present time, which are for the most part readily available and accessible to the urban researcher. Records of the future are those records that are presently under the aegis of the Office of Records Management of the National Archives and are physically located in our federal records centers, our Suitland, Maryland, annex, or still with the agency of origin. The designations of past, present, and future as used in this paper are arbitrary designations and are only intended as a possible approach to records of urban value in our custody. First we will examine some nineteenth-century records of possible urban research value in the National Archives.

Two recent examples of the use of nineteenth-century records in the custody of the National Archives appeared in the serial publication, *Historical Methods Newsletter* of the Department of History, University of Pittsburgh (vol. 3, no. 2 [March 1970], pp. 2–14). This publication is devoted to the quantitative analysis of social, economic, and political development. The first article is entitled "Town Populations in the Early United States Censuses: An Aid to Research" by Edward K. Muller of the Department of Geography, University of Wisconsin, Madison. The second example is an article entitled, "Postal Records as an Aid to Urbanization Studies" by Richard W. Helbock, Department of Earth Science, New Mexico State University.

Muller's article demonstrated how the manuscript or original federal population census returns, 1820–60, can be used for estimating town populations not otherwise shown for western, southern, and back-country sections of the United States in the first half of the nineteenth century. As Muller shows in his paper, the published versions of United States federal census failed to do an adequate job in reporting the populations of the smaller towns. This study was devoted to towns in Indiana and Ohio, and statistical tables accompany the article, which shows among other things the difference in results between the published and manuscript censuses.

The article on postal records compared two small towns in Oregon five miles apart, one of which became part of a new railroad line in 1884, while the other town was bypassed. Obviously the town on the railroad line grew while the other declined. The writer demonstrates by a comparison of certain data in the postal records with the population figures of the two towns that the researcher can gain further insight into the nature of the growth of one town and of the decline of the other. For example, the records of the compensation of postmasters give details beyond those available in the census records about when one town surpassed the other in growth. The records in the National Archives used in these two studies were series among the records of the Post Office Department and the Bureau of the Census. As Muller stated in his article, he used the manuscript census returns. The paper on postal records was based on the series designated Records of Appointments of Postmasters. These records have a date scope from 1815 to 1929.

The Appointments of Postmasters series contains the following information about United States post offices: date of establishment (usually the date when the first postmaster was appointed and occasionally the date when the post office began operations); date each succeeding postmaster was appointed; changes in the name of the office (and the relevant date); date office was discontinued (or reestablished, if this was applicable); and the name of the post office to which the business of the discontinued office was sent. Other postal records of possible value in nineteenth-century urban research are the Reports of Site Locations, 1867–1946. These reports are completed forms submitted by postmasters giving the exact location of their communities; geographical information, including data about nearby rivers, creeks, railroads, landmarks; and other information. Since these reports are dated and contain the information described, they provide useful clues in pinpointing smaller urban and town areas not to be found elsewhere.

To return to the original federal population census schedules, it should be pointed out that the returns from 1850 forward contain ethnic, economic, and sociological (i.e., educational) information about the persons enumerated. Using census and postal records together, many quantitative studies are possible for small urban entities in the nineteenth century. There are finding aids or preliminary inventories available which describe series furnishing additional data or useful information on this subject, but time does not permit their discussion here.

Some other possibilities of nineteenth-century urban research in the National Archives are customs and immigration passenger lists, photostatic copies of records of naturalizations in New England courts, and records of the government of the District of Columbia.

The National Archives has more or less complete passenger arrival records for certain East Coast and Gulf ports such as Baltimore, Boston, New Orleans, New York, and Philadelphia. The customs passenger lists begin with the year 1820 (there are baggage lists giving passengers' names for Philadelphia, 1800–1819) and continue until the end of the nineteenth century, at which time the immigration passenger lists begin. Basically, both types of lists contain the same information. In addition to the name of the passenger, they show age, sex, occupation, place or origin of birth, port of embarkation, and in some cases the exact name and address of the passenger's ultimate destination in the United States. These records, then, contain certain ethnic and social information, are of value in tracing migration patterns, and should provide the urban searcher insight about changing demographic patterns in East Coast port cities. These lists and accompanying indexes are available on microfilm.

Among the records of the Immigration and Naturalization Service in the National Archives are photostatic copies of records in New England courts (federal, state, and local), 1787–1906, and accompanying indexes. These records show, in addition to the applicant's name, the date and place or court of naturalization, his occupation, country of birth (sometimes the exact place of birth), date of birth, the length and places of residence in the United States prior to naturalization, and occasionally the date and port of his arrival in this country. These records were used as part of research for a supplemental paper, which is available to this group, discussing immigration in Boston.

The records of the government of the District of Columbia contain information that reflects the economic, social, ethnic, and political growth of the District of Columbia. (Again, these records can be used in conjunction with published and manuscript census returns in quantitative and statistical studies.) For example, there are tax and assessment records, 1824–98, and similar series which trace the economic growth of the city. There are other series which trace the various changes in governmental structure. In addition there are records of the Georgetown city government (long a separate entity within the District of Columbia) with tax and assessment records as early as 1800. In the Washington National Records Center there are 551 volumes of deed books to real property in the District of Columbia, 1792–1869. There are other records in the National Archives Building relating to the District of Columbia, such as buildings and legislative records, but these have only ephemeral value for urban research and little or no value for population research. There are housing records for the District for a later period which will be discussed later.

The records discussed here are selected examples of urban population research possibilities in the National Archives for the nineteenth century.

Our federal government was not so involved in state, local, and personal affairs as it was to be in the twentieth century. Since I have discussed only demographic aspects of urban research possibilities, I feel that other facets of urban research can be found among other nineteenth-century records. In considering other nineteenth-century possibilities the urban researcher should consider what federal agencies were involved at urban or town levels, how and when they were involved, the nature of the agency's records as to informational content, and the feasibility of research. For example, records of the Internal Revenue Service, Customs Service, the Treasury Department, and federal courts offer future possibilities in our area of interest.

Federal records and sources of the twentieth century that can be used for urban population research are more fruitful than nineteenth-century federal sources because:

1. As already noted, the federal government became more concerned with the welfare of its citizens, and primarily as a result of this agencies were created with the beginning of the New Deal era. This had the effect of creating useful records and reports.

2. The need of the agencies for necessary demographic data and the improved methods of technology for producing and assimilating this data make the task of the quantitative and analytical researcher easier than it would be if he were using nineteenth-century records.

3. The creation of the National Archives and Records Centers, contemporaneous with the creation of many of these records, helped personnel in agencies that accumulated these records and in the National Archives and Records Centers become conscious of and anticipate future research needs.

Some of the richest sources of urban population data in the National Archives are the various groups of federal housing records. Since a paper on these records is to be presented later, I will only briefly refer to them here. Some of the record groups available to the urban researcher containing population and related data are the Records of the United States Housing Corporation, 1917–52; Records of the Federal Housing Administration, 1932–50; General Records of the Housing and Home Finance Agency, 1933–54; Records of the Office of the Housing Expediter, 1942–53; Records of the Federal National Mortgage Association, 1938–54; and Records of the National Capital Housing Authority, 1934–51. Not only are these records interrelated as to informational content, but also their bureaucratic and administrative histories show an almost inextricable intermingling. These records reflect not only population data but also social, economic, and ethnic information. For example, the records of the United States Housing Corporation are records of an agency that began in World War I as an agency to provide housing, local community transportation, and other community facilities for industrial workers. In the course of their operations many reports, statistics, and correspondence were assembled which reflect urban population and housing conditions, especially in New York and Pennsylvania.

An outstanding example of population data can be found among the cartographic records of the Records of the Federal Housing Administration. The record series selected is entitled Graphs Summarizing Characteristics of Selected Urban Areas, 1900–1938. This series was examined in detail to show data that can be found in housing records. There is a graph showing the shifts in the location of the fashionable residential area in six American cities from 1900 to 1936 (i.e., Boston; Seattle; Minneapolis; San Francisco; Charleston, West Virginia; and Richmond, Virginia). There is a national graph showing the value of new urban residential building compared with urban residential rents and factors affecting urban population growth covering the years 1920–40. Several bar graphs show the distribution of mixed racial blocks according to percentage of nonwhite families from representative northern cities for the year 1934. There are also bar graphs showing percentages and numbers of Negroes in northern and southern cities for the year 1930. Another graph shows the percentage of increase in population of thirty-five American cities with a population under 250,000 and thirty-five American cities with a population over 250,000 for the decade from 1920 to 1930. The foregoing are but selected examples of records in this series, which is but one series in one record group of housing records in the National Archives.

Two sources of useful urban population data are the records of the Women's Bureau, 1918–56, and the records of the Children's Bureau, 1912–40. The Women's Bureau, established in the Department of Labor in 1920, is responsible for bettering the working milieu of the wage-earning woman. The Women's Bureau in the course of its activities has compiled and collected statistical information, analyses, and reports that are rich in social, economic, and educational information that cannot be found elsewhere about women in cities. The Children's Bureau, which began in the Department of Commerce and Labor in 1912, is now part of the Department of Health, Education, and Welfare. The urban researcher can find data on infant and maternal mortality, working mothers, the birth rate, orphanages, juvenile delinquency, desertion, dangerous occupations, accidents, child diseases, and state and community measures for the protection and care of children. Related records can be found in the Records of the Department of Commerce, Records of the Department of Labor, and Records of the Department of Health, Education, and Welfare in the National Archives.

In Record Group 220, Records of Presidential Committees, Commissions, and Boards, is the so-called Kerner Commission Report dealing with urban disorders in 1967. The many reports and studies that went into the creation of this report are an invaluable source of specialized sociological and population data.

There are many records in the National Archives that have not been mentioned but that are similar to those discussed above. These are records dealing with housing, welfare, and labor. My purpose has been to suggest some urban population possibilities to the researcher and, I hope, to stimulate additional studies. I have not mentioned the relation or impact of the depression and World War II on urban population; however, the special supplemental papers available to this group should help fill these gaps.

The records of the welfare agencies that were established in the 1960s offer possibilities for research. The accumulation and the statistical manipulation of demographic data and other data relevant to urban areas are necessarily part of the activities of these agencies. This is borne out by the preliminary descriptions of their records that are in the Washington National Records Center, some of which will go to the National Archives. Three record groups that especially contain such data are the Records of the Economic Development Administration, the Records of the Office of Economic Opportunity, and the Records of the Neighborhood Youth Corps. These record groups have in common the fact that their data pertain to the lower economic strata of our society. They document the ever-increasing federal concern with individual welfare. Because of their nature these agencies must of necessity produce more and more published reports, statistics, and other information. This proliferation is a boon to the urban researcher and makes Weber's 1899 sources sketchy by comparison. We must not lose sight of the original unpublished source material, however, for it is susceptible of further statistical analysis and interpretation.

PANEL ON HOUSING

One-third of a Nation: The Dilemmas of America's Housing, 1607–1970

RICHARD O. DAVIES

Seldom has a national problem been so fashionable as the current "crisis of the cities." With dependable regularity, the television networks produce a special documentary; and the news and opinion journals report endlessly upon the interrelated problems of poverty, pollution, crime, law enforcement, racial tensions, inadequate social services, disintegrating educational systems, declining revenues, and the loss of leadership to the suburbs. By the mid-1960s, no serious aspirant to high public office dared enter the political wars without a well-defined program to deal with the "urban crisis."

Not to be outdone in either quantity or quality, the universities greeted the urban crisis with enthusiasm. Several major universities established new courses, workshops, and research programs. Consequently, the several social sciences cooperated long enough in their interdisciplinary programs to produce that curious hybrid called the urbanologist. This new action-oriented scholar presumably possesses the perspectives of the historian, the cultural insights of the anthropologist, the technical skills of the political scientist, and the statistical certainty of the sociologist.

While the journalists, politicians, and professors tried to convince each other that an urban crisis did in fact exist and that somebody ought to do something about it, those few lonely souls who call themselves urban historians enjoyed a private chuckle. For they had heard it all before.[1] They knew that the urban crisis even predated Pat Moynihan and Walter Cronkite. In fact, they recognized a persistent and unhappy theme of American urbanization that stretches back at least 150 years. Further, if one reads between the lines of Carl Bridenbaugh's magnificently researched—if somewhat tediously written—histories of colonial cities, the time span can readily

1. But the historian also failed to anticipate the great concern of the 1960s. In a sharp critique of the literature of urban history, Prof. Richard Wade told his fellow scholars that "It cannot be said that when the public turned to historians they got much help . . . when the public needed us, we were not there." Philadelphia, April 1969, Organization of American Historians.

be extended an additional 100 years.[2] Just as the contemporary American is concerned about crime in the streets, so too was the eighteenth-century Bostonian and nineteenth-century New Yorker. As any student of America's urban history knows, poverty, congestion, pollution, racial violence, inadequate transportation, proliferating slums, and hopelessly ineffectual governments were the outstanding features of the nineteenth-century American city. The urban problems that plague us today are not markedly different than those of 100 years ago.[3] They have just grown bigger with the expanding urban population. In fact, as Edward Banfield's recent book argues, it might be that our urban environment is actually substantially better today than at any other time since the Civil War.[4]

There is a numbing quality of continuity and endurance—an unhappy sense of failure—to our urban heritage. It is essentially a history of neglect compounded by inadequate and unimaginative response. As Prof. Sam Warner has observed, "To an historian, twentieth-century urban America presents a picture of endlessly repeated failures. The problems of the American city have been known for a very long time; yet they persist. Novelists, social critics, settlement workers, and reporters in the early 1900s painted a reasonably complete portrait of urban America."[5]

This dreary record of inadequate response to obvious social needs is vividly evident to those few scholars who have researched various aspects of the history of America's urban housing. Just as the role of housing is central to the current urban crisis, so it was 100 years ago. In fact, it was the rapidly deteriorating working-class housing areas that first attracted the attention of journalists and social workers. Michael Harrington pointed to the dismal housing of the urban poor of the 1960s, and Franklin Roosevelt talked about "one-third of a nation ill housed" in 1937; Jacob Riis poignantly wrote about "how the other half lives" in 1890, while Philadelphia charity workers in 1846 described the incredibly sorry living conditions of that city's poor.[6] Even the small colonial cities had their "mini" slums, and not

2. Carl Bridenbaugh, *Cities in the Wilderness* (1938; reprint ed., New York: Capricorn Books, 1964); *Cities in Revolt* (1955; reprint ed., New York: Capricorn Books, 1964).

3. For example, see Constance McLaughlin Green, *The Rise of Urban America* (New York: Harper & Row, 1965); Blake McKelvey, *The Urbanization of America, 1860–1915* (New Brunswick: Rutgers University Press, 1963) and *The Emergence of Metropolitan America, 1915–1966* (New Brunswick: Rutgers University Press, 1968); and Charles N. Glaab and A. Theodore Brown, *A History of Urban America* (New York: Macmillan Co., 1967).

4. Edward Banfield, *The Unheavenly City* (Boston: Little, Brown & Co., 1970).

5. Sam Bass Warner, Jr., *The Private City: Philadelphia in Three Periods of Its Growth* (Philadelphia: University of Pennsylvania Press, 1968), p. ix.

6. Michael Harrington, *The Other America* (New York: Macmillan Co., 1962); Jacob Riis, *How the Other Half Lives*, ed. Donald Bigelow (New York: Hill & Wang, 1957); Gilbert Osofsky, "The Enduring Ghetto," *Journal of American History* 55

only have these pockets of poverty endured, but they have expanded a thousandfold. American cities, thus, have always had an acute housing problem. Significantly, despite the many outraged cries from today's ahistorical social critics, the available evidence shows that our urban housing problem is less serious than at any other time during the past 100 years.[7] The major source of poor housing in America today actually lies beyond the scope of this paper—in rural and small-town America, not in metropolitan America. Fully 60 percent of all American substandard housing exists today in villages or rural areas.[8]

There is no definitive history of American urban housing, although within the past ten years scholars have made a creditable beginning; several important monographs and articles now stand on the library shelves. Perhaps even more important, the sister social sciences have contributed much to our understanding of contemporary housing, especially as related to the poor and racial minorities. But much remains to be done.

The most pressing need is for a new perspective. Housing is merely the product of many larger forces and processes of urbanization, but one of the major weaknesses of housing reform efforts until the 1950s was the basic assumption that poor housing *created* other social disorders rather than merely being part of a general poverty syndrome.[9] This point of view has now largely disappeared, and it is generally recognized that it is impossible to isolate the category of housing from the more general category of urban affairs. Housing research to the historian has meant primarily the history of housing reform. Reflecting their own social commitments, historians have concentrated largely upon the activities of reformers and their legislative struggles. One can find more written about public housing, slum clearance, tenement laws, and experimental communities than other housing topics. More recently, as a reflection of the "black revolution," scholarly attention increasingly has been directed toward the history of housing discrimination and the creation of racial ghettoes.

(September 1968): 243–55. For a description of an urban slum prior to the Civil War, see Oscar Handlin, *Boston's Immigrants* (1941; reprint ed., New York: Atheneum, 1966), pp. 100–114.

7. Banfield, *Unheavenly City*; U.S., Department of Housing and Urban Development, *1967 Statistical Yearbook*, p. 41.

8. The *1967 Statistical Yearbook* shows that 60 percent of all substandard housing in the United States is located in rural areas and communities of less than 2,999 inhabitants. Further, 38 percent of all urban substandard housing exists in cities of less than 50,000 inbahitants. Substandard housing is defined as "all dilapidated units, plus deteriorating and sound units lacking one or more plumbing facilities."

9. For a discussion of this problem, see Roy Lubove, *The Progressives and the Slums* (Pittsburgh: University of Pittsburgh Press, 1962), pp. 245–56, and Richard O. Davies, *Housing Reform during the Truman Administration* (Columbia: University of Missouri Press, 1966), pp. 138–40.

While this reformist orientation has produced important studies, it creates an unfortunate imbalance in our perspective of America's housing. By focusing upon merely one aspect of housing policy, the reform-minded researcher inadvertently has created the impression that this is about all there is to the history of American urban housing. But the fundamental and enduring truth is that today barely 1 percent of the nation's housing is publicly owned or operated and that federal housing has been relatively insignificant in meeting the nation's housing needs.[10] The overwhelming percentage of America's housing in 1970, as in 1870 or 1670, has been built, financed, and owned by private interests and individuals.

The basic determinant in the development of American urban housing from colonial times to the present has been private developers seeking to maximize their profits with little or no concern for the greater public interest. It has been a heritage of individual Americans seeking the best possible shelter in the best possible location for themselves and their families. The essential and basic factor in America's housing, past or present, is that it is the creation of private capital and private ambitions. This is because the American urban community was the creation of private capital, and its form and functions were designed primarily to facilitate the acquisition of private wealth. As Professor Warner has observed,

> Under the American tradition, the first purpose of the citizen is the private search for wealth; the goal of a city is to be a community of private money makers . . . the successes and failures of American cities have depended upon the unplanned outcomes of the private market. The private market's demand for workers, its capacities for dividing land, building houses, stores and factories, and its needs for public services have determined the shape and quality of America's big cities. What the private market could do well, American cities have done well; what the private market did badly, our cities have been unable to overcome.[11]

It is within this broader context, then, that the student must approach the history of America's housing—both its successes and its failures.

Before the much-needed synthesis of the nation's housing can be written, fundamental questions need to be formulated and basic research needs to be accomplished. Who built America's housing? What regional differences and national similarities are readily evident? How did slums develop, and

10. The approximate number of public housing units operative in January 1970 was nine hundred thousand. The approximate total number of housing units in the United States at that same time was 60 million.

11. Warner, *Private City*, p. x.

why has society been so reluctant to recognize their existence and the special considerations that they require? Who were the land developers? How did their social values differ from the housing reformers? Why has local government played such a passive role in the process of urban growth? Did zoning laws reflect a victory for the urban reformer, or were they in reality a shrewd "triumph of conservatism" engineered by local land developers?[12] Why has the housing construction industry remained so fragmented, so unwilling to incorporate new technological and mass production methods?[13]

Specifically, we need local, regional, and national studies of both housing legislation and housing development. Scarcely no other industry has had more direct impact upon the way Americans live than the so-called housing industry, but it has almost entirely eluded the historian. We do not have a single useful study of a large real estate promoter. We know virtually nothing about the history of housing construction. We need solid local histories on housing promoters and planning and zoning boards. On the national level we are without a useful study of the so-called real estate lobby; it has been much criticized but largely ignored by researchers.

Finally, we need to reexamine our assumptions and conclusions about the federal housing programs. Can the government's efforts in housing be classified as reform (as I blandly assumed in my study of the politics of public housing)?[14] Perhaps the more central role of the federal government's efforts has been not to provide housing for the poor, but rather to facilitate the scramble for wealth on the part of the private housing industry. Do key administrators in the federal housing bureaucracy share primarily the assumptions of the reformers or the industry?[15] Who administers national policies locally? Because most federal housing policies must originate on the local level, studies from the bottom up seem especially appropriate.

The difficulties and challenges for mature scholarship in the history of housing are staggering. The first step is for research libraries to begin to collect systematically the papers and records of local housing agencies, planning commissions, and real estate developers, as well as those of national leaders, pressure groups, and federal agencies. Once these mountains of material become available, then the scholar is going to have to demonstrate considerable ingenuity in handling the raw data. For example, it would seem

12. The author acknowledges his indebtedness to the central theme of Gabriel Kolko's *Triumph of Conservatism* (Glencoe, Ill.: Free Press, 1963).

13. The historian would do well to consult the general reference work by Glenn H. Beyer, *Housing and Society* (New York:Macmillan Co., 1965); for this reference see pp. 117–248.

14. See Paul Conkin's review of *Housing Reform during the Truman Administration*, in the *Journal of American History* 53 (December 1966): 642–43.

15. On the surface the answer seems to be both. For one study of a leader during the Truman era, see *Housing Reform during the Truman Administration*, pp. 129–30.

to be an overwhelming chore to follow the endless thousands of real estate transactions for a particular neighborhood as it changed its economic functions and ethnic compositions over the years. But until it is done, how can we describe with certainty the actual process of urban change? With the much-proclaimed information storage and retrieval capabilities of the modern electronic computer, perhaps such important studies are now within the realm of possibility.

Professor Warner's pioneering study of Boston's suburban development in the final three decades of the nineteenth century, however, provides us with important methodological insights.[16] His *Streetcar Suburbs* shows not only how private concerns determined the decline of Boston's central core, but also the shape of her working-class suburbs. By placing the data of three decades of real estate transactions upon computer cards, Warner reduced a heretofore unmanageable mass of statistics to an understandable pattern. His utilization of similar techniques to demonstrate the advantages to urban historians of comparative studies (in this case Philadelphia at three points in its development) is replete with significance for those who seek to study local and national housing topics.[17] In these two bench mark studies Warner has demonstrated how the urban historian can blend his traditional research methods with those of the social scientist.

Warner's studies also provide a central theme that future housing students might employ with profit as their primary frame of reference: the American city as the product of innumerable separate private decisions. Consequently, the nature of urban housing has also been the product of these individual decisions—of the developer, the builder, the businessman, the politician, and the citizen. It was out of the pervasive influence of private capitalism and an aversion to central planning and quality control that the interrelated social disorders of our contemporary city emerged. As Professor Warner concludes from his study of Philadelphia, "Privatism left the metropolis helpless to guarantee its citizens a satisfactory standard of living. Privatism encouraged the building of vast new sections of the city in a manner well below contemporary standards of good layout and construction. . . . In short, the industrial metropolis of 1930, like the colonial town, and the big city which had preceded it, was a private city and the public dimensions of urban life suffered accordingly."[18]

For the sake of convenience, the history of American urban housing can be categoried into three major eras: The Era of Laissez Faire (colonial times to the late nineteenth century); the Era of Minimum Standards (1880 to

16. Sam Bass Warner, Jr., *Streetcar Suburbs* (Cambridge: Harvard University Press and M.I.T. Press, 1962).
17. Warner, *Private City*.
18. Ibid., p. 202.

the New Deal); and the Era of Limited Federal Intervention (1930 to the present). Although imprecise and open to challenge on several particulars, this loose scaffolding at least affords a semblance of order and continuity.

The first period is the one about which we know the least. It is also the most important, for by the late nineteenth century, except for some western and southern cities, the basic pattern of the American industrial city had been established. Even the automobile would not dramatically change the basic urban plan, except by accelerating the already established movement to the suburbs. What needs to be kept in mind is that the federal government, except in unusual circumstances, played only a marginal role in the life of the average American citizen until well into this century. Living in partial isolation, whether on the farm, in one of the many small "island communities" that dotted the landscape, or in a self-contained urban neighborhood, the nineteenth-century American went about the business of seeking to improve his own condition. The national government played almost no role whatsoever in the structuring of our cities.[19]

By the time the automobile arrived, most urbanites with sufficient funds had already established the familiar pattern of today's urban housing. Those who were able abandoned the older central areas of the cities for the outer fringes; they did so partly because the high land prices in the heart of the city drove them out, and life far removed from the business and industrial areas seemed more pleasant. When they left the central city, their housing was occupied by the newly arrived urbanite—the European immigrant—and when his descendants began to move up in status and out in location, the black American from the rural South moved in. And there we are today.[20]

The crucial and seemingly instinctive decision of the nineteenth-century middle class American to flee to the suburbs instead of staying and repairing his existing housing set the pattern for our contemporary housing picture. Outward migration has been the central theme of the process of urban growth for more than one hundred years. Successive waves of technological advances—the horsecar, the electric trolley, and finally the automobile—meant that the city could expand in ever-widening concentric circles. The physical boundaries of the nineteenth century "walking city" were forever

19. I am indebted to Robert Wiebe's *The Search for Order* (New York: Hill & Wang, 1966), for the "island community" concept; see Seymour Mandelbaum, *Boss Tweed's New York* (New York: John Wiley & Sons, 1965), pp. 1–39, for a useful discussion of communications theory and the decentralization of New York in the post–Civil War era. For a concise, but extremely useful survey of the forces that created American cities, see Glaab and Brown, *History of Urban America*, pp. 1–166.

20. There is an extremely large amount of literature on this topic. The most useful interpretation drawn from that massive set of materials is Banfield, *Unheavenly City*, pp. 23–44. For the critical period of the late nineteenth century, John Garraty's chapter on the cities in *The New Commonwealth* (New York: Harper & Row, 1968), pp. 179–219, is especially useful.

shattered.[21] By the advent of the twentieth century, the urban crisis was already very much at hand. The privatism of America's urban civilization had produced the working-class tenement and ethnic-racial ghetto. In the central areas of the city, the poor were snared and the institutionalization of the slum occurred. In short, the scramble for private wealth and power had indelibly sculptured the shape of the urban community and divided the urban population between the core and the suburbs.[22]

Ever since the colonial era, of course, individuals had bemoaned the plight of the urban poor and called for remedial action. But it was not until the late nineteenth century that sufficient numbers of individuals became fully aware of the dimensions of the problem. As a result of this new social awareness there emerged modern American social reform. It sought means to ameliorate the unsavory conditions created by an urban industrial society, and the housing reform movement emerged from this larger reform impulse that coalesced during the late nineteenth century under the general name of progressivism.[23] Immediately, the attention of the new urban reformer was drawn to the tenement in which the poor somehow survived. The ensuing conflict between the reality of deplorable conditions and a deeply engrained self-help ideology resulted in the moderate concept of imposing by law minimum standards upon urban housing. Social workers, journalists, ministers, and other concerned private citizens joined forces to eliminate the most objectionable aspects of the tenements by means of inspection laws that required sufficient light, air, and water for the inhabitants, as well as a reasonable number of water closets and fire escapes.

This embryo stage of housing reform has drawn the attention of several capable scholars. Allen F. Davis, Louise C. Wade, and Robert H. Bremner have placed the housing reforms of the Progressives into the larger intellectual, social, and political contexts.[24] Roy Lubove, especially, has provided us with a definitive study of the single, most important reform effort—that of Lawrence Veiller and the creation of the New York Tenement

21. McKelvey, *Urbanization of America*, pp. 75–85.

22. This standard interpretation has become so common that it is practically a cliché. It must be kept in mind, however, that our contemporary American suburbs contain many working-class citizens and also many impoverished Americans. This is especially true of cities of less than 100,000 in population.

23. The most useful studies that develop this particular interpretation are Eric Goldman, *Rendezvous with Destiny* (New York: Knopf, 1956); Richard Hofstadter, *The Age of Reform* (New York: Knopf, 1955), pp. 172–212; and George Mowry, *The Era of Theodore Roosevelt* (New York: Harper & Row, 1958), pp. 59–105.

24. Allen F. Davis, *Spearheads for Reform* (New York: Oxford University Press, 1967), pp. 60–102; Louise C. Wade, *Graham Taylor: Pioneer for Social Justice* (Chicago: University of Chicago Press, 1964), pp. 58–82; Robert H. Bremner, *From the Depths: The Discovery of Poverty in the United States* (New York: New York University Press, 1956), pp. 205–12.

House Commission.[25] This state law of 1901 provided a model for minimum standards legislation, and by 1920 over forty other cities had similar commissions and codes. The total impact of this legislation was marginal at best, and by 1920 the state of the nation's urban housing was worse than in 1901.[26] Nonetheless, as Lubove concludes, the pioneering work by Veiller and his associates provided "a permanent legacy" for future government activities in urban housing.[27]

As concern for the housing conditions of the urban poor grew during the early part of this century, increasing numbers of Americans joined in the growing, but amorphous housing reform movement. City planners, social workers, economists, sociologists, elected officials and journalists, among others, sought new solutions to the perplexing housing dilemma. Not surprisingly, however, in view of the strong agrarian tradition in American thought, many simply gave up on the industrial city and looked expectantly —and naively—toward the clean and green countryside as future sites of housing for the industrial worker. Inspired by the garden city concept of that visionary Englishman, Ebenezer Howard, many reformers advocated the construction of completely new, planned residential communities.[28]

Spearheading this essentially antiurban housing reform movement was the Regional Planning Association, an informal organization of planners, architects, and social critics. Their two attempts at providing the working class with decent housing in a good environment resulted in failure, for their expansive plans raised the prices beyond the reach of the workingman. Radburn and Sunnyside, however, provided the inspiration for the greenbelt programs of the Resettlement Administration during the 1930s. Especially useful for an understanding of this phase of housing planning are Professor Lubove's extended essay on the RPA and Paul Conkin's thoughtful and expertly executed study of the many communal and cooperative programs of the New Deal.[29] However exciting these visionary and agrarian-inspired plans might have been, they proved to be simply nothing more than unrealistic dreams to a society not given to economic and social engineering.

While the historians have written extensively of these few—and ineffectual —reform efforts, they have almost totally ignored the movement that did

25. Lubove, *Progressives and the Slums.*

26. Glaab and Brown, *History of Urban America,* p. 177.

27. Lubove, *Progressives and the Slums,* p. 148.

28. The literature on this topic is vast, but for a useful summary see Glaab and Brown, *History of Urban America,* pp. 289–300, and McKelvey, *Emergence of Metropolitan America,* pp. 47–48. For an interesting alternative of the planned industrial suburb, see Stanley Buder, *Pullman* (New York: Oxford University Press, 1967).

29. Ray Lubove, *Community Planning in the 1920's: The Contribution of the Regional Planning Association of America* (Pittsburgh: University of Pittsburgh Press, 1963); Paul Conkin, *Tomorrow a New World* (Ithaca: Cornell University Press, 1959).

more than anything else to provide more Americans with adequate housing—the movement to suburbia. Contrary to general impressions, the housing left behind in the central city more often than not was not substandard, and when families left for suburbia, that housing then became available for lower-income families. While Clarence Stein and Rexford Tugwell were assembling Radburn and Greenbelt, the thousands of George F. Babbitts located in every American city were making a tidy profit in promoting their innumerable Glen Oriole Estates located far from the dirty factories and the overcrowded immigrant tenements. Their social motivation might have been nil, but in the final analysis, these individual realtors and promoters succeeded far better than the visionary planners in improving markedly the total housing picture in the United States.[30] Scott Donaldson has recently produced a useful study that places the suburb within the context of American intellectual history, but he does not attempt a study of the suburbanization process; this extremely important topic still awaits a talented historian.[31]

The economic disaster of the 1930s provided the political impetus for the emergence of the final stage of American housing policy—the Era of Limited Federal Intervention. The New Deal provided the transition from the minimum standards concept of the Progressives to the more advanced concepts of public housing and slum clearance. As Clarke Chambers has shown, during the 1920s many social reformers had moved to the position that minimum standards legislation was a failure due to the difficulties in getting local governments to enforce them.[32] Seizing upon the model of the United States Shipping Board's residential construction program during the World War, they developed the concept of public housing.[33] Franklin Roosevelt, however, could not have cared less, and it was only through the dynamic efforts of Sen. Robert F. Wagner that the 1937 Housing Act was passed. At the heart of the bill was the "equivalent elimination" provision which required the construction of one unit of public housing for every substandard dwelling place destroyed. Public housing, in short, originally was firmly tied to slum clearance.[34] The study by Timothy McDonnell provides us with an

30. For an appreciation of the dimension of suburban growth, see Glaab and Brown, *History of Urban America*, pp. 281–90, and McKelvey, *Emergence of Metropolitan America*, p. 154. For a sociological study of the archetype suburb, see Herbert Gans, *The Levittowners* (New York, Knopf, 1967). The census of 1970 will show that approximately 70 million Americans live in suburban areas.

31. Scott Donaldson, *The Suburban Myth* (New York: Columbia University Press, 1969).

32. Clarke Chambers, Seedtime for Reform (Minneapolis: University of Minnesota Press, 1963), pp. 131–38.

33. Roy Lubove, "Homes and 'A Few Well Placed Fruit Trees': An Object Lesson in Federal Housing," *Social Research* 27 (Winter 1960): 469–86.

34. Robert Moore Fisher, *Twenty Years of Public Housing* (New York: Harper & Row, 1959), pp. 206–8.

understanding of the complexities of the legislative process, and J. Joseph Huthmacher's biography of Senator Wagner effectively relates the New Deal housing legislation to his urban liberalism hypothesis.[35]

Although this supposedly dramatic departure has attracted several sympathetic scholars, the most important housing legislation of the Roosevelt era has gone almost totally unnoticed. This is, of course, the establishment of the Federal Housing Administration in 1934. Created as an emergency attempt to resuscitate the moribund housing construction industry, by 1945 it had become institutionalized as a permanent federal agency. Its function was to facilitate the construction of new housing for the middle class by insuring mortgage loans, thereby eliminating most risk from the lending institutions and making it easier for the growing middle class to build new housing on the city fringes.[36] In 1944 Congress took this program one step further when it passed the Serviceman's Readjustment Act, one portion of which established a program that guaranteed low-interest housing loans to qualified veterans.[37]

As a direct spin-off of the New Deal housing adventures, the Truman administration inherited an allegedly comprehensive housing legislative program that had been concocted during the war years by an unlikely coalition of New Dealers and Robert Taft.[38] Recognizing the political importance of housing legislation and successfully exploiting the postwar housing shortage for political advantage, the Truman administration succeeded in passing the program in 1949.[39] The heart of the program was the inauguration of a massive urban redevelopment program and the construction of 810,000 units of public housing. An important symbolic feature of what most scholars call the most single important housing bill ever passed by Congress was the adoption of a national housing policy that established the goal of "a decent house in a good environment for every American family." Significantly, the new slum clearance and urban redevelopment program was freed from public housing; it is interesting to note that one of the most ardent defenders of the private lending and construction groups, Sen. John W. Bricker, supported the new slum clearance urban redevelopment program while simultaneously fighting public housing with great vigor and imagination.[40]

35. Timothy McDonnell, *The Wagner Housing Act* (Chicago: Loyola University Press, 1957); J. Joseph Huthmacher, *Senator Robert F. Wagner and the Rise of Urban Liberalism* (New York: Atheneum Publishers, 1968).

36. Paul Conkin, *The New Deal* (New York: Thomas Y. Crowell, 1957), p. 62.

37. Davis R. B. Ross, *Preparing for Ulysses* (New York: Columbia University Press, 1969), pp. 89–124.

38. Richard O. Davies, "Mr. Republican Turns 'Socialist': Robert A. Taft and Public Housing," *Ohio History* (Autumn 1964), pp. 135–43.

39. For an understanding of the impact of the postwar housing shortage, see Ross, *Preparing for Ulysses*, pp. 238–74.

40. Bricker is quoted by Scott Greer, *Urban Renewal and American Cities* (Indian-

Thus, the federal housing policies have largely worked at cross-purposes, and it is the urban poor who have come up the losers. While FHA encourages the white middle class to move to suburbia (and until the 1960s flatly discouraged the blacks to do so via its discriminatory underwriting policies), slum clearance provided land developers with a profit to destroy unsightly (but oftentimes adequate housing) in the central areas. As Scott Greer bluntly puts it, "At cost of more than three billion dollars the Urban Renewal Agency has succeeded in materially reducing the supply of low-cost housing in American cities."[41] The redevelopment of areas produced civic centers, office buildings, and lovely parks while the poor had to seek housing elsewhere. Meanwhile, the federal government reneged on its public housing pledges; by 1968, those 810,000 units promised in 1949 still had not been constructed.[42]

Public housing has proved extremely disappointing to its early enthusiasts. First, lukewarm support on the local and national levels melted before the determined and resourceful opposition of the real estate lobby and its conservative allies. This strong opposition has prevented any massive public housing program from developing.[43] Those projects that have been constructed, however, have frequently drawn considerable criticism from the left. Michael Harrington, for example, succinctly summarized this concern in *The Other America*. Public housing, he writes, has failed "to solve the problem of the slum, and above all, the problem of slum psychology." The reason for this has been the physical segregation of public housing from the rest of the urban society, thus reinforcing the images of poverty and social failure among the inhabitants. "One must balance the physical improvements (and hopefully, the consequent improvement in health) against the new forms of alienation," he concludes.[44]

Historians of the future will find much to study during the 1960s. The Kennedy and Johnson administrations produced five important housing bills. Although the sixties will be viewed as a decade of experimentation in housing (such as the Model Cities program and rent subsidies), the legislation was nonetheless firmly rooted in the liberal tradition of the New

apolis: Bobbs-Merrill Co., 1956), p. 17. Davies, *Housing Reform during the Truman Administration*, provides a study of the politics that resulted in the Housing Act of 1949. Leonard Freeman, *Public Housing: The Politics of Poverty* (New York: Holt, Rinehart, & Winston, 1969), provides a useful study of the role of public housing in local and national politics. A classic study of the role of public housing in one city (Chicago) is Martin Meyerson and Edward C. Banfield, *Politics, Planning, and the Public Interest* (Glencoe, Ill.: Free Press, 1955).

41. Greer, *Urban Renewal and American Cities*, p. 3.
42. Department of Housing and Urban Development, *1967 Statistical Yearbook*, p. 243.
43. Freedman, *Public Housing*.
44. Harrington, *Other America*.

Deal. It sought to correct some obvious injustices, but no attempt was made to alter the existing private housing system.[45]

Certainly one of the most timely topics for modern historians is the black urban ghetto. The considerable work done by sociologists in recent years overwhelmingly demonstrates the difficult problems confronting the black American in the cities. Karl and Alma Taeuber's excellent study of residential segregation conclusively documents the pervading climate of racial prejudice existing in our cities. Segregated housing, they conclude from their enormous amount of quantitative evidence, is pervasive throughout the nation, and it "not only inhibits the development of informal, neighborly relations between whites and Negroes, but insures the segregation of a variety of public and private facilities."[46] As Andrew Billingsly points out, housing segregation is the "chief external badge of inferiority" suffered by black Americans.[47] To be certain, the housing situation for black Americans has improved tremendously—the number of substandard urban dwellings inhabited by blacks has decreased markedly. Although the statistics are encouraging, the gap between white and black Americans nonetheless remains great.[48]

In this critical area, we especially need the long view provided by history. The pioneering efforts by Gilbert Osofsky and Allen Spear provide solid models for future research.[49] What is needed from the perspective of this paper are studies of discrimination on the local level by landlords, realtors, and developers. The reinforcement of local discriminatory policies by the federal government—especially the FHA—should prove to be an exciting topic to a reform-minded scholar. What is needed, of course, is a comprehensive history of the Negro in the twentieth-century city, but before it can be attempted, much monographic work needs to be done.

The historian who surveys the more recent era, however, will have to deal with the paradox that as the nation's housing situation improved, the level of criticism also increased. Contrary to the assumptions of those who

45. For a concise summary of the housing legislation of the 1960s, see Morton J. Schusshein, *Toward a New Housing Policy* (New York: Committee on Economic Development, 1969), 64 pp.

46. Karl and Alma Taeuber, *Negroes in Cities* (Chicago: Aldine Publishing Co., 1965), p. 1.

47. Andrew Billingsly, *Black Families in White America* (Englewood Cliffs, N.J.: Prentice-Hall, 1968).

48. See Banfield, *Unheavenly City*, pp. 33–34, for a discussion of this important development.

49. Gilbert Osofsky, *Harlem: The Making of a Ghetto* (New York: Harper & Row, 1966); Allen Spear, *Black Chicago: The Making of a Negro Ghetto* (Chicago: University of Chicago Press, 1967). An essential source for all students of black urban life is, *The Report of the National Advisory Commission on Civil Disorders* (New York: Bantam, 1968).

enlisted in the antipoverty wars of the Great Society, the existing system of an essentially private system with limited federal intervention has been systematically eliminating the amount of substandard housing at a fairly rapid pace; within the past twenty years the amount of substandard urban housing has been sliced in half, and one seemingly reasonable projection sets 1980 as the probable date when the goal of a decent house for every American family might well be realized.[50] Scholars looking at the housing situation following 1949 might very well keep in mind Edward Banfield's caveat that the urban crisis might very well be more the product of our ever-escalating expectations than it is the result of actual deprivation.[51]

The broad outline of the history our nation's housing from colonial times to 1970 has thus been sketched, but the sources for it are scattered in innumerable books and articles. Still, considerable monographic work is needed, especially on regional and local topics, and the talents of a mature and perceptive scholar are needed to draw the sources together into a much-needed synthesis. The scholars need, however, the assistance of research librarians and archivists. They must acquire and process the essential research materials. Especially important are the papers of key government officials, but local research facilities should also make a concerted effort to acquire and make available to researchers the papers of local realtors, land developers, and builders. The records of local zoning and planning commissions, as well as of key city officials, should yield invaluable data about the processes of urbanization. Local history can add a most important dimension to our knowledge about the complexities of urban growth and urban change. In fact, those books most often singled out by students of urban history as being especially significant are tied directly to particular cities.

Although much research needs to be accomplished, the broad outline of the nation's housing is clear enough. The heritage is essentially one produced by a system of private capital that has penalized the poor. The fundamental political and social assumptions of the American people have precluded any massive federal intervention into the housing field. The gains of the past half century have resulted largely indirectly from the expansion of suburban areas which has made available acceptable—if older—housing in the central city for the nation's less affluent. That the number of substandard houses is rapidly dwindling is evident to anyone who consults the demographic evidence, but from the long view of 300 years of urban expansion, what is

50. William Grigsby, *Housing Markets and Public Policy* (Philadelphia: University of Pennsylvania Press, 1963). For example, between 1950 and 1960, the number of substandard housing units was sliced by 40 percent. See Bernard Freeden, "Housing and National Urban Goals," in James Q. Wilson, ed., *The Metropolitan Enigma* (Cambridge: Harvard University Press, 1968), pp. 266–67.
51. Banfield, *Unheavenly City*, p. 19–22.

painfully evident is that substandard housing for a substantial segment of our urban population has been a central part of our heritage. That it still endures is unhappily the case.

Federal Urban Housing Programs
and Data

HENRY B. SCHECHTER AND
ELIZABETH K. SCHOENECKER

As a participant in the conference on urban research, I am pleased to describe the data and records generated by federal urban housing programs. All too often people engaged in housing research are not aware of the existence of data that would be of value to them. Or, they may needlessly spend too much of their limited time hunting for information because they do not know the sources. I realize that the latter situation can be frustrating to somebody outside the federal establishment who is not familiar with the mysterious and often-changing web of the federal housing organization. My presentation will aid those who are particularly interested in housing data. I do not intend to present a laundry list of data and sources. I will touch upon the significance of certain types of information and indicate the related groupings of data that are produced through various programs.

Before I discuss the federal housing programs themselves, I would like to provide some perspective on their place in the overall picture of national housing production.

In fiscal year 1969, 1.6 million new units were added to the housing supply, in addition to about four hundred thousand mobile home units. The bulk of the 1.6 million new units, almost 1.3 million units, was conventionally financed, that is, with no federal subsidy, insurance, or guarantee. Of the approximately three hundred thousand new units under government programs, about one hundred eighty thousand (or 60 percent) were subsidized, while the others had only loans insured or guaranteed by the federal government. Thus, federal housing programs account for less than 20 percent of the new units added to the housing stock in fiscal year 1969. And, only three-fifths of these were subsidized.

The role of the federal mortgage loan insurance and guaranty programs (FHA, VA, and Farmers Home Administration) in the existing home purchase market is probably more significant. We really do not know exactly

56

how significant that role is because nobody has a good measure of the total number of housing units that change ownership or occupancy each year.

The production and acquisition of housing units is supported by a variety of programs. These programs can be divided into general categories. This division will help to explain the kinds of data generated by the programs and the availability of that data. I am including only the Department of Housing and Urban Development program and other primarily urban programs and will not discuss the housing programs of the Department of Agriculture.

The HUD housing production programs can be divided into three general categories: public housing, the subsidized private programs, and the insured but unsubsidized programs. Public housing, as its name implies, is owned by a public body, a local housing authority. It serves low-income families and elderly and handicapped individuals whose incomes do not exceed the limits set for the area in question, limits which are related to the cost or rent of standard housing in the area. This program is a "deep subsidy" program. The legislation creating it specified that it was to serve families in the lowest income group: families who cannot afford to pay rentals high enough to cause private enterprise to build an adequate supply of decent, safe, and sanitary housing to serve them.

The second major grouping of HUD production programs includes those units which are privately owned but still subsidized so as to allow their owners to charge tenants rentals lower than market rate, and, in the home-ownership program, to make possible lower monthly mortgage payments than would be possible with an unsubsidized mortgage. The major programs included in this group are the rent supplement program and the so-called Section 235 and Section 236 programs. In each case, the units are planned, constructed, and financed privately, although they meet certain standards which are required by the FHA for insurance coverage. The rent supplement program is intended to serve those in the same income levels as low-rent public housing. The tenant pays 25 percent of his monthly income as rent; the balance needed to make up the true economic rent for the unit is paid to the owner by the Department of Housing and Urban Development. This payment is the rent supplement. As a tenant's income rises, his share of the rent also rises and the subsidy decreases. When his income exceeds the income limits, he is not required to move, as in public housing, but instead must assume the full economic rent himself. Thus, there can be subsidized and unsubsidized units in the same building.

Sections 235 and 236 refer to "shallow subsidy" programs. They serve a group whose income cannot exceed 135 percent of the public housing income limits set for the area. Thus, they serve families in a somewhat higher income group than those served by either public housing or rent supplements. These families have incomes too high to make them eligible for the deep subsidy programs, but still not high enough to enable them to afford decent housing on the private market.

Section 235 is a home ownership program and Section 236 is a rental program, but their interest-rate subsidy mechanisms are similar. Again, in each case the units are privately planned, built, owned, and financed. The Section 235 units built for home owner occupancy are produced by builders who can sell the homes either to buyers eligible for subsidy or to those who require no subsidy. Section 236 rental projects, as in the projects of rent supplement housing, may be sponsored by a nonprofit, limited-dividend or cooperative organization. (The Section 236 program is replacing the 221(d)(3) program, and it provides a deeper subsidy.) In all cases, the housing must meet certain standards set by the FHA for insurance coverage.

The third general category of urban housing programs is the insured but unsubsidized group. The units are the FHA-insured and VA-guaranteed homes with which we are all familiar and also the units in multifamily projects covered by regular rental housing mortgage insurance. The government insurance which backs these mortgages enables lenders to finance units with lower down payments and longer repayment periods than is possible with conventional financing. There is no subsidy involved, however. The borrower repays the full principal and interest, as well as a mortgage insurance premium.

In addition to housing production programs, HUD also has programs to promote the rehabilitation of units. Under the Section 115 program, direct grants of up to $3,500 can be made to low-income home owners in federally aided urban renewal areas, in concentrated code enforcement areas, and in certified areas (which need substantial rehabilitation to bring their homes up to required standards and for which applications for federal assistance for urban renewal or concentrated code enforcement will be submitted within three years). Also, rehabilitation loans at reduced interest rates can be made to persons in renewal, code enforcement, and certified areas. These loans and grants are made on the premise that it is worthwhile, socially and economically, to subsidize rehabilitation that will decrease the need for demolition and total urban renewal.

Rehabilitation can also be undertaken with FHA-insured loans, both subsidized and unsubsidized. Again, recipients of the subsidized insured loans must have incomes which do not exceed the income limits set for their area.

And last, 1965 legislation authorizes the local housing authorities to purchase and rehabilitate existing housing that can be rented to low-income families. Just as in newly constructed public housing, annual contributions from HUD to the local housing authority cover the principal and interest payments on these units. Annual contributions may also be used to subsidize the occupancy by low-income families of units in private housing structures that are leased by local housing authorities.

Several other HUD programs are also of interest because they affect the environment in which housing units are placed and because they generate data about that area. These are the Model Cities, the 701 Comprehensive Planning, the Community Renewal, and the New Communities programs.

The Model Cities program is an interagency effort under HUD leadership, with state and local government and private citizen groups, to make a concentrated attack on the social, environmental, and physical problems of a neighborhood. Programs developed by the local Model Cities agency and private citizen groups are funded in one of two ways: (1) with categorical program grants available from the specific federal agencies and (2) with supplementary grants awarded by HUD to finance programs included in the comprehensive plan which are innovative or for which no program grants are available.

Under the 701 Comprehensive Planning program, grants of two-thirds[1] of the cost of preparation of comprehensive development plans can be made to state, metropolitan, and regional planning agencies, organizations of public officials; cities; counties in redevelopment areas; multistate regional commissions; official governmental planning agencies for federally impacted areas; localities that have suffered a major disaster; and areas that have suffered a decrease in employment from declining federal purchases or closing of a federal installation. These grants enable the planning agencies to prepare general and functional plans, to program capital improvements and to coordinate all related plans and activities of the state and local governments. These activities may cover such subjects as land use, transportation, water and sewers, open space and recreation, housing, health, education facilities, and other aspects of physical and human development and governmental management that can be improved by long-range planning and coordination.

Planning for a better urban environment is also done with funding from the Community Renewal program and with planning advances under the regular urban renewal program. The Community Renewal program provides grants to county or municipal public bodies of up to two-thirds of the cost of preparing a renewal strategy for a locality. The program identifies

1. Three-fourths of the cost is granted when the applicant is (1) in a redevelopment area or economic development district designated by the secretary of commerce under Title IV of the Public Works and Economic Development Act of 1965; (2) in a local development district, certified under Section 301 of the Appalachian Regional Development Act of 1965; (3) in a federally impacted area; and (4) in one of the various regional commissions established by the Appalachian Regional Development Act of 1965 or under the Public Works and Economic Development Act of 1965.

slums or deteriorating areas; measures the nature and degree of blight; determines which financial, relocation, and social resources are needed to renew the area; and prepares programs of action for the community to take in the ensuing five-to-ten-year period.

A relatively new program which could greatly affect the urban scene in coming years is the New Communities program. The building of new, self-contained, viable communities, rather than new subdivisions of already-existing cities, is a relatively new phenomenon in the United States. But this form of urban development is stirring up a great deal of interest, and we probably will see more new communities started in coming years. At present, HUD's direct role in encouraging new communities is limited to guaranteeing the financial obligations of developers of new communities of up to $50 million for a single community. It can also make available to the local community supplementary grants, in addition to regular program assistance for such projects as sewer and water systems and open-space development. Proposals are presently being drawn up for more direct participation in the future.

Now that I have briefly described the programs, I can describe the types of data that they generate. Basically, the housing production programs generate two kinds of data—data about the characteristics of occupants and data about the characteristics of the units themselves.

In the public housing program, data on occupants are collected at two different times—at the time of application for admission and during annual reexaminations to determine continued income eligibility. The characteristics covered include such things as: the age of the head of the family, the number in the family, the number of workers, the number of minors, the income, rent, race, and the public and private assistance or benefits received. For both admissions and reexaminations, these data are compiled by the local housing authorities and transmitted to HUD for each unit in the projects. HUD summarizes the data on tenant characteristics and publishes them annually for the entire United States and for each HUD region. Selected data are also available for individual local housing authorities.

Information on the development progress and selected characteristics of the low-rent public housing program is available primarily from the *Low-Rent Project Directory*, which is published annually by HUD. This report is intended primarily for departmental use but is available on request. It lists projects by state, HUD region, local housing authority, and locality.

Information about the projects includes the number of units in each project according to status—i.e., number of units in the preconstruction stage, in the construction stage, and under management. Information on the number of units by bedroom size is available in the reports on occupancy characteristics that I mentioned earlier. Data on development and other unit costs, some of them broken down by HUD region, are available in the *HUD Statistical Yearbook*. More specific information about a particular project or about the projects in a particular locality would have to be obtained from the local housing authority, which owns and manages the units.

Data on characteristics of the occupants and the units under the subsidized private programs are obtained from the applications forwarded to HUD by project sponsors. These applications are not available for research purposes, since individual families are identified by name on them. But summaries of the characteristics are prepared from samples of the applications and are available from the FHA Division of Research and Statistics under the assistant secretary for Housing Production and Mortgage Credit. The characteristics are those one would expect on an application which is used to determine eligibility for subsidy—income, number in the family, rental expense, etc. On rent supplement housing, these reports have been prepared several times since the program began in 1965.

On Section 235 housing, such summaries are prepared quarterly. They, too, are available from the Division of Research and Statistics. Soon they will be incorporated in the quarterly *FHA Trends* reports, which have a wide mailing distribution among market researchers, manufacturers, builders, and universities. A great deal of published information is available on the unsubsidized FHA-insured home mortgages, and somewhat less information is available for the unsubsidized project mortgages.

On the home mortgages, data are available both on the occupants and on the units themselves. Occupant data include the ages of the mortgagor and his wife, the income, the years of marriage, and the number of dependents— all the factors which would be requested on the application to determine the applicant's ability to carry the mortgage. Data on the unit and on the mortgage are even more extensive—one can check up on loan/value ratios, on costs of real estate taxes and insurance, monthly maintenance bills, and utilities expenses. If he is interested in the housing units insured, the researcher can obtain figures on the market price of the site, the number of stories, the building material used, the number of bedrooms and bathrooms, and the presence of various appliances such as dishwashers or garbage disposals, among other characteristics. All of these and other characteristics are outlined in the quarterly *FHA Trends* reports on the home mortgage and property improvement loan programs. For those persons interested in comparative or localized profiles, as are many market researchers and manufacturers who avail themselves of the *Trends* reports, the data are also available by state and even by major local area in the quarterly reports.

Three annual publications are also helpful: the FHA *Annual Statistical Summary*, which presents national data; *Data for States and Selected Areas,* which provides characteristics of cases for states and localities; and a report on insurance operations in each state, county, and Standard Metropolitan Statistical Area (SMSA).

The data which I have mentioned so far have been generated directly for, or as a result of, a government housing program. But there is a great deal of other housing data related to more than just the programs in which the government is involved. As I mentioned in the beginning of my presentation, federal housing programs account for only a fraction of national housing production; the bulk of our housing comes from private unsubsidized construction. Therefore, in discussing the nation's housing needs and supply, we at HUD must be concerned with the economic and social factors that influence private construction.

The most complete picture of the housing stock, of course, comes from the decennial census of housing. The main problem with this is that after a few years most of the data becomes obsolete. In the interim between housing censuses, though, the Bureau of the Census does publish current housing reports based on sample surveys which cover many facets of the housing stock; e.g., occupancy-vacancy data, type of tenure, housing quality, number of rooms, etc.

We also try to keep tabs on the current market picture through a variety of surveys, many of them undertaken for HUD by the Bureau of the Census. For example, the Census Bureau publishes monthly construction reports which keep us abreast of the number of new units started in both single-family and multifamily structures, inside SMSAs and outside SMSAs, and by census regions. We are interested not only in the number of units started, but also in the rate at which they are absorbed by the market and their prices. To obtain this data, HUD and the Bureau of the Census jointly publish a monthly sales-price survey on the number of one-family homes built for sale and the number sold during the month and their median sales price. And HUD and the Census Bureau are now releasing data quarterly from a market absorption study covering the rate at which new units in multifamily projects are rented by unit size and rental classes. As a byproduct of the housing starts survey, HUD and the Census Bureau are now publishing a new monthly series on housing completions, which provides information on the number of new privately owned and publicly owned housing units completed each month. All of this information is published or released to the press and is available to the public.

Market information is also available from the analyses of particular housing market areas made by the Federal Housing Administration. These reports on the prospective demand or occupancy potential for housing in a particular area are prepared primarily to guide HUD—and specifically FHA—operations, but are also available to builders, mortgagees, and others concerned with housing problems and trends in a particular area. The reports include estimates of the numbers of various kinds of subsidized and unsubsidized housing that could be absorbed in the area annually for a two- or three-year period.

In addition to market data, we are also interested in the financial data relating to housing. The high interest rates and scarce mortgage credit of the past year and the resultant drop in housing starts have pointed up dramatically the importance of financing to the housing industry.

A new Mortgage Loan Gross Flows reporting system, set up under HUD coordination and inaugurated recently, will soon provide periodic data on the amount of mortgage loans purchased, originated, and sold by each of the major mortgage lending groups and on commitments made for new mortgage loans. The data are being compiled for one-to-four-family homes and apartment houses, with separate figures on FHA, VA, and conventional loans and on nonresidential properties and farms. The statistics given for construction loans are distinguished from the statistics for long-term loans; and, in loan originations, the statistics for new housing are distinguished from those for existing housing. This kind of mortgage market information is another tool we hope will warn of credit stringencies such as those of 1966 and the past year. The monthly mortgage gross loan data will be available to researchers from the HUD Office of Economic and Market Analysis.

Historical data comparable to that which will be collected has been estimated by the Office of Economic and Market Analysis and is available in a HUD publication entitled *Mortgage Loan Gross Flows,* from either the HUD Information Center of the Government Printing Office. Information on other characteristics of mortgage loan transactions, such as interest rates, average purchase price, loan amount, and years to maturity, can be obtained from various periodicals such as the *Federal Reserve Bulletin* and the *Journal of the Federal Home Loan Bank Board,* which are published monthly. Summary data on FHA-insured mortgage programs are set forth in a monthly HUD publication, *Housing and Urban Development Trends.* Similar data on VA-guaranteed home loans can be found in a VA publication, *Loan Guaranty Highlights.* They are available from the statistics offices of HUD and the VA.

The *HUD Statistical Yearbook* presents a historical compilation of these financial data, as well as historical data on housing production and sales, housing quality, occupancy and vacancy rates, construction costs, and other general statistics related to housing and urban development. This compendium, which can be quite useful for urban researchers, is sold by the Government Printing Office.

So far, most of the data sources I have described are unanalyzed, dry statistics. HUD has also published a number of research reports which present cross-sectional analyses of the occupants of various types of housing units. For example, a publication entitled *Housing Surveys, Parts 1 and 2,* contains a survey of the occupants of new housing units and a survey of mobile homes and the housing supply.

The survey of the occupants of new units provides information about the occupants of newly constructed units (both owners and renters), characteristics of the units, and characteristics of the units occupied previously. This kind of data helps in improving our understanding of the linkages in the market between new and existing housing; it helps us to better understand the changes in one part of the market that result from changes in another part. Likewise, the mobile homes survey, by describing the characteristics of mobile home owners and of their units, helps us to better understand the contribution made by this form of shelter in meeting the nation's housing needs. We found, for example, that most owners of mobile homes rely on them as their primary residences—less than 5 percent of the surveyed mobile home owners had second homes. The cross-sectional data are, of course, as of one point in time.

The two studies were published in one volume, available from either the HUD Information Center or the Government Printing Office. At the present time, another survey of the occupants of new units is being made. When completed and analyzed, it will give us more current information on this group and will provide us with a source of comparison with the previous survey. After it is published this survey will also be available from the HUD Information Center. That office stocks copies of all research reports published by HUD, as well as other HUD publications. In addition, the personnel in that office can assist in locating data which are available on request from the operating units of HUD, some of which I have mentioned, but which are not generally distributed in the Information Center.

The work we have done on quantifying housing needs is still another source of available data and analysis. Reports on traditional housing market analysis speak of housing demand. Since incomes are not always sufficient to create effective demand, it becomes apparent that housing demand cannot always be equated with housing need. Housing need is often more extensive than housing demand.

Therefore, to estimate a realistic number of units needed to adequately shelter every American household, we found it necessary to consider housing expense-to-income relationships and to estimate how many of the needed units will have to be subsidized in coming years.

The total number of new units needed is based on several factors—the number needed to house additional households, to permit an increase in vacant units, to compensate for demolitions and other casualty losses, to permit removal of the balance of dilapidated units, and to replace mobile homes that are scrapped.

We began doing these estimates for the congressional hearings on the

Housing and Urban Development Act of 1968, which proposed a ten-year national housing goal of the construction or rehabilitation of 26 million housing units, with 6 million of them to be subsidized. That goal was promulgated by the president and the Congress in the 1968 act. The legislation also called for an annual report to the Congress on the progress made in realizing the goal.

The first annual report was submitted by the president in January 1969 and the second in April 1970. In addition to reestimating the need for each of the various components of the housing supply and detailing the progress made in achieving the goals, the annual reports estimate the amounts and availability of the various inputs needed for housing construction—land, construction labor, construction materials, and mortgage financing. These reports are printed by the Banking and Currency Committee of the House of Representatives and are available from the Government Printing Office.

All of the programs or data I have described thus far bear directly on some aspect of housing itself—availability, need, costs, and other characteristics. But in the beginning of my talk I also mentioned some HUD programs which influence the environment in which housing is placed. These programs also generate data and reports which may be useful to urban researchers.

As in the housing production programs, the structure of the program determines the type of data generated and from whom it will be available. The Model Cities program, for example, stresses the role of the local government and citizens groups in formulating an outline of the physical and social problems they want to correct and of the proposed programs to be used. Thus, a great deal of the data about the workings and experiences of the programs in a particular model city would have to come from the information office of the local Model Cities agency.

Work is now progressing on development of a national information system into which all the local systems would feed information. The data will be statistical data on the city and the model neighborhood as well as program status information. It will be taken from the program plans of the applicants, from the monthly and quarterly reports the model cities are required to submit, and from the Census Bureau and other survey information about the cities.

As the system becomes operational in the next few months, two kinds of products are envisioned. A data retrieval system will be set up to make data about a specific city available on request. This service is expensive, and, at least initially, it will probably not be available outside the government. Secondly, recurring reports and city profiles will be published giving certain statistical and program data about the model cities. This source, too, may have limited availability at first, but could probably be tapped for special research projects.

The Model Cities Service Center technical bulletin is a medium for the exchange of ideas and experiences among Model Cities directors and may also be helpful to researchers. It also covers recent speeches by Model Cities' policy-making officials, pertinent legislative and administrative changes, and Model Cities involvement by federal departments and agencies other than HUD. This monthly bulletin is put out by the Model Cities Service Center of the Conference of Mayors/National League of Cities and is available from them on request.

Community Renewal is a grant program designed to facilitate planning of a community's renewal strategy. In the action program which is produced, problems are defined, solutions are proposed, and courses of renewal action are recommended. Since problems of blight vary from locality to locality and the resources to combat them also vary, the reports will vary a great deal in content.

The general topics covered, however, will be much the same. For example, a report by a Community Renewal program describes the blight in various defined study areas and details the structural and environmental conditions. Various other data would also be given about the areas, such as present and projected population mix, housing trends and needs, industrial and commercial acreage trends, and the economic basis for renewal. The report might describe existing land use patterns and propose new patterns. Also, the types of renewal projects proposed for specific areas would be set forth—code enforcement for some, rehabilitation for others, and complete clearance and redevelopment for still others. Where this involves displacement of households and businesses, a relocation workload program would be prepared.

For each city for which a grant has been made and the study completed, a complete copy of the Community Renewal program with all its map and technical appendixes is on file at the HUD central office, as well as in the HUD regional office for the HUD region of the city. Generally, these reports would be available for use in the office by a researcher, but extra copies are not available for distribution by HUD. The city agency which coordinated the study would, of course, be the best source of information; and it would print extra copies of the studies for distribution.

The reports and data generated by the Comprehensive Planning Assistance program, commonly called the 701 program, are widely available. All the documents produced with 701 funds (whether for a small area or a metropolitan, regional, or statewide area), are public property and are available for research. HUD guidelines require that a copy of each report, study, plan, and map be submitted to the HUD library in Washington, to the HUD regional office in the region in which the planning area is located, to the twelve depository libraries, to a designated state library, and to the federal clearinghouse operated by the Department of Commerce. The specific libraries are designated in a HUD publication entitled *Comprehensive Planning Assistance Handbook II,* available from the HUD Information Center.

In addition, when a state agency draws up the 701 program, the documents are often submitted to all the college libraries in the state. And most metropolitan and regional planning commissions are beginning to establish their own libraries and include 701 programs in their holdings. The 701 reports on deposit at the various libraries are available only for reference. Personal copies may be purchased from the federal clearinghouse or from the local or state agency which produced the report.

A typical 701 report might actually consist of a number of studies on various subjects, for example, a traffic and thoroughfare plan, a school plan, population projections, studies of development goals and policies, a capital improvements program, a land use plan, or studies of housing needs, among others. Thus, for each grant recipient there may be a number of documents on file in the depository libraries. Since 1968, there has been a statutory requirement that each 701 planning effort shall contain a "housing element"; the newer planning reports, therefore, should begin to produce some extensive local housing data.

The New Communities program, having been authorized only since 1968 in the Housing and Urban Development Act, has not thus far generated much data. But the idea of creating new cities to absorb some of the nation's growth and thus take off some of the pressure from existing cities is rapidly becoming a reality. Already, as you know, several "new towns" have been started right in this area.

Literature is not lacking on new towns in general. The New Communities staff at HUD has compiled and published an annotated bibliography on the subject. Published in December 1969, the bibliography covers foreign as well as American new town experiences. It is available from the HUD Information Center or from the Government Printing Office. Another source of information which actually lists all the large developments and new communities completed or under construction in the United States since 1947 is the January 1970 issue of *Urban Land,* a monthly publication of the Urban Land Institute. That entire issue is devoted to the question of dispersal as the answer to urban overgrowth.

These, then, are basic data sources on some of the federal programs that affect the course and quality of urban development and that produce data. I have mentioned some of them here even though they are not strictly housing programs because housing and urban development do proceed hand in hand.

Useful data are also produced by private, government-sponsored institutions that are indirectly supported by the government. For example, the Federal Home Loan Bank System, a private, government-sponsored institution, and the Federal Savings and Loan Insurance Corporation, which are affiliated with the Federal Home Loan Bank Board, are very important in the housing picture. In the aggregate, the savings and loan association members of the Federal Home Loan Bank System, whose deposits are insured by the FSLIC, are the leading source of residential mortgage financing in the country. The Federal Home Loan Bank Board publishes a number of statistical series on housing finance related to mortgage-financing transactions of conventionally financed homes; i.e., homes for which the mortgages are not insured or guaranteed by the federal government. These series are in the *Journal of the Federal Home Loan Bank Board*. Other statistical series appear in the Federal Home Loan Bank Board news releases put out periodically by FHLBB Office of Public Affairs.

The Federal National Mortgage Association is another government-sponsored private corporation which facilitates the workings of the mortgage market. FNMA operates as a secondary market for the purchase and sale of FHA-insured and VA-guaranteed mortgage loans. The extra liquidity thus injected into the market is especially important in a tight money situation such as we have been experiencing.

Prior to the Housing and Urban Development Act of 1968, FNMA was a government corporation that had special assistance and other functions, as well as responsibility for the secondary market operations. Since the 1968 legislation, FNMA has become a private corporation. A new government corporation, the Government National Mortgage Association, was created to take over the special assistance and management and liquidating functions, while FNMA retained the secondary market functions. Under this new arrangement, FNMA and GNMA activities are covered separately in such HUD publications as the monthly *Housing and Urban Development Trends* reports and the *HUD Statistical Yearbook*. In addition, FNMA publishes the *Federal National Mortgage Association News*, a biweekly summary of its activities and of mortgage prices.

This brief look at the various data sources connected with the urban housing programs gives the researcher some idea of the types of data which are available and where they can be found.

Some Aspects of Urban Housing Records in the National Archives

JEROME FINSTER

In this paper I shall try to cover the highlights of certain aspects of records in the National Archives that pertain to housing. The information presented here can be only introductory at best. For this reason, those who require more details should examine our relevant issuances and consult with our staff through either correspondence or personal interviews. Our subject specialists have knowledge of these records that far surpasses what is ordinarily committed to print. Indeed, for this conference, some of that information has been put into print, and it appears in the staff papers that have been distributed to you. Two of these papers—those by Katherine H. Davidson and Kathryn M. Murphy—are concerned specifically with housing records; and several other papers, while they are focused on other records, contain observations about their housing-related aspects. The information in these staff papers and in the National Archives records inventories are convenient bases on which inquiries for further details can be made.

Obviously, the history of American housing cannot be written entirely or even principally from federal records; nevertheless, the characteristics of those records are such that they merit consideration as often complementary and sometimes unique sources, particularly in respect to developments of the past half century. I shall outline some of these characteristics today—specifically origins, types of data content, and availability.

It is appropriate to consider the origins of the records because knowledge of these may effect our judgment as to whether or not material is likely to contain information useful for research. The functions assigned to each federal agency in large measure dictate the kinds of records that it accumulates. But the creation, modification, and termination of agencies and the distribution and the redistribution of their functions have tended greatly to complicate the administration of their records. For this reason, although a researcher may—and should—have at the outset of his work an informed notion as to those agencies whose records are likely to be relevant to his inquiry, he will in most cases need further information about them to track down their records in the administrative jungle of the United States government. There is considerable information about the functions and the organization of the older agencies in the Brookings Institution monographs of a generation ago, and Praeger has published so far about a dozen volumes on various bureaus and departments. Nevertheless, neither of these series examines agency structure very deeply, so that the lines to records accumulations are often not readily discernible. In many cases, therefore, the researcher will have to depend on the archivist and on National Archives descriptive finding aids for details about agency development and for guidance as to likely research materials.

The housing records, as all records in the National Archives, are organized on the basis of record groups, each of which usually comprises the records of a bureau-level or departmental-level agency. Looking at the roster of National Archives record groups, one perceives that nine denote records of agencies concerned principally or entirely with housing. None of these agencies was in existence before World War I, for it is only within the past half century that the federal government has concerned itself broadly with the provision and facilitation of housing. Some of the agencies represented by these record groups are no longer in existence because either their programs have been completed or abandoned or they have been absorbed into other agencies that continue their functions. Further, some of the agencies that have given their names to the record groups derive from earlier agencies, some of whose records they have absorbed. To sum up, we have agencies, sometimes independent, sometimes integral parts of others, spanning the years from World War I to the present, whose names include (among others) the United States Housing Corporation, the Public Housing Administration, the Federal Housing Administration, and the Department of Housing and Urban Development. The aggregate volume of their archival materials in the National Archives is about thirty-three hundred cubic feet, but two of these nine record groups refer to agencies that had a jurisdiction over only the District of Columbia, and the volume of their records is only twenty-five cubic feet.

But there are many more record groups that contain information of interest to researchers in housing. By one count there are at least twenty-three such record groups, and these represent agencies whose functions cover a broad sweep of concerns—legislative, research, fiscal, economic, and even military. It is in respect to these agencies probably more than in respect to the housing agencies that knowledge of functions and activities is necessary for an assessment of the potential of their records as sources useful for research. Examples that illustrate the diversity of these record groups are the records of the Reconstruction Finance Corporation, the United States Senate, the National Resources Planning Board, and the Freedmen's Bureau.

The records have several characteristics that derive from their origins. First, being largely products of federal programs that were conducted in and that concerned many places, they in sum contain a concentration of data about many places that cannot be equalled at other depositories. The detailed data that I shall mention later are usually in files that are organized on the basis of local area within each state and federal region. This organization facilitates geographically oriented research. Until the installation of a country-wide system of data transmission by electronic means permits researchers readily to obtain information from distant sources, a large collection of records about a large number of places is a great convenience, whether the researcher must visit the depository or the depository is willing to furnish copies. Second, there are among the records many nonfederal materials—for example, press clippings, reports, maps, and statistical tabulations—organized by locality or subject, whose preservation by copy at local depositories is often doubtful. These materials were accumulated by the federal operatives as sources of information. Apart from their interest for their data content, they may be important as evidence of the stimuli that may have affected federal policy and the conduct of programs. Third, many of the records that relate to the administration of programs for federal assistance in connection with housing include documentation of rejected alternative decisions. History cannot be written entirely in terms of what might have been, but what did take place is often better understood if we know why something else did not happen.

The time span of the archival housing records is principally the period from World War I to the present. The extant records of the United States Housing Corporation, which produced about six thousand houses for workers in defense industries, total about 450 cubic feet and cover the years 1918–52, but the records after the early 1920s chiefly concern the financial liquidation of the agency and its properties. The United States Shipping Board of the same era sought to provide housing (for shipyard workers), and perhaps one hundred cubic feet of its records are relevant to that program. Active federal interest in housing was not reborn until the Great Depression. Since that unhappy event there have been a multitude of federal housing programs. Public housing, slum clearance, mortgage insurance, and rent control are among the concepts now very familiar to us.

For the eras before World War I there are relatively few records, but these should nevertheless be mentioned. As a heritage of early federal tax legislation, we have the direct tax lists for the state of Pennsylvania among the records of the Internal Revenue Service. These have been reproduced on twenty-four rolls of microfilm and contain descriptive and other data relating to dwellings in that state as of 1798. The functions of the Treasury Department and the Freedmen's Bureau have resulted in records containing principally financial data about houses in certain cities in the Confederacy.

One caveat before we turn to descriptions of the data in the housing records: the attribution of a defunct agency's name to a record group does not necessarily imply that all of its records have been accounted for by either transfer to that group or destruction. Rather, since government seldom yields any functions, some of these records are among the store of paper currently held by successor agencies or in their National Archives record groups. To a large extent, records documenting policy decisions in the housing agencies are still retained in current files, but the degree of their archival transfer often depends on the files schemes under which they are organized. Simply put, the extent to which files of one era are separately maintained from those of another affects the feasibility of their transfer. But this is only one factor associated with records maintenance techniques that ultimately bear on archival holdings. I mention this point because the role of the National Archives in respect to federal records should be understood to include its records management function, which is to insure that government files are maintained efficiently and at the same time to afford adequate documentation of policy, programs, and social phenomena.

While the National Archives cannot be said to have comprehensive policy documentation of all housing agencies in the modern era, we are currently engaged in a major program to accession such material. Within days we have received from HUD over three hundred cubic feet of files in the period 1946–68 that were maintained by the successive administrators of the Housing and Home Finance Agency and the first departmental secretary. Also, we are presently devising plans for the selective retention of records of the various program offices of HUD.

Although the documentation of policy formulation is not comprehensive in the National Archives, the actual working out of policy as exhibited in ad hoc actions is documented by case files that are available for many programs. This point will be demonstrated by some of the descriptions that follow.

The data that appear in the housing records can be grouped into four broad categories: (1) information about dwellings as physical entities; (2) information about the residents of the dwellings; (3) economic information; and (4) information about social factors. Information about dwellings as physical entities relates to their descriptions, their materials of construction, their facilities and the services available in them, evidence of deterioration, and maintenance practices. Information about the residents includes statistics regarding their number, racial or national origins, and composition by income class or work occupation. It sometimes also includes the names of the occupants or the owners of the dwellings. The economic information relates to the value, costs, and prices of dwellings, credit, insurance, and other financial data (subsidization and rentals and sales). The category of social factors includes the subsumed conditions in the community that are illustrative of the state of its housing; the role of local, state, and federal governments in providing for housing; and the sentiments about housing.

For no category or subcategory of information are there enough data in the archival records to render them the sole source to be relied on. But there is a great variety of useful information in these archives, despite their uneven coverage. Let us now look at examples. We begin with the information about dwellings as physical entities. The Pennsylvania direct tax lists of 1798 contain descriptions of dwellings and their adjunct buildings, including the number of their stories and windows and their dimensions. Unfortunately, the National Archives has no such lists for other states and information concerning the whereabouts of only a few. Jumping a century, we find photographic slides of the era from 1895 to 1905 in the records of the Public Housing Administration. These slides are descriptive of slum housing in several cities of the United States and in some cities abroad.

The Bureau of Labor Statistics record group contains questionnaires of uncertain origin, circa 1905, that have much information about housing in a neighborhood in Chicago. The number of rooms in each dwelling is one of the points covered. The records of the United States Housing Corporation of World War I and the early 1920s include items descriptive of the housing sponsored by that agency; there are architectural sketches, maps, blueprints, photographs, slides, and textual matter. The National Bureau of Standards collected records for the 1920s on the statistics of construction for various types of dwellings, methods of planning for housing, and standardization and prices of building materials.

The project case files in the records of the Public Housing Administration provide descriptions of the Public Works Administration housing of the 1930s. Construction plans for the three Greentowns of the New Deal are available in two record groups—Records of the Public Housing Administration, Record Group 196, and General Records of the Department of Housing and Urban Development, Record Group 207. The Federal Housing Administration records of the late 1930s show on a block basis data for many cities in respect to the number of housing units, baths, toilet facilities, and the number of buildings constructed before 1919. The FHA records of the period 1936–46 include over three hundred samples of insurance files that contain architectural plans and specifications. Among the records of the Public Building Service, an agency normally associated with the maintenance of federal government buildings, there are photographs of temporary housing of World War II. And in the records of the State Department, of all places, there are photographs of 1950 vintage that illustrate techniques in housing construction. Building materials used in dwellings are described in the Pennsylvania direct tax lists and in the records of the Rent Control Commission of the District of Columbia of the period 1919–25.

The 1905 questionnaires in the Bureau of Labor Statistics record group describe flooring in dwellings and indicate the presence or absence of plaster. The facilities available to residents in emergency World War I housing for shipyard workers are described in the Shipping Board records. The PHA records describe the sanitary (or unsanitary) conditions prevalent in dwellings that the proposed housing was intended to replace. The features and services found in rental property were among the bases of permissible rents under the controls of the World War II and Korean periods; these are documented in the records of the Office of the Housing Expediter. There may be some special technical interest in blueprints of electrical distribution systems found in the records of the United States Housing Corporation.

The principal source of information about the deterioration of urban housing is the series of block-data maps of the Federal Housing Administration for the period 1934–39. The files of the District of Columbia Rent Commission also contain some details on this point and about maintenance (or lack of it) by landlords.

Information about the racial or national identification of residents appears in several collections: namely, the 1905 BLS questionnaires; the District of Columbia Rent Commission files, which also register complaints about discrimination in housing; the block-data maps of the FHA Real Property Inventory; and the PHA project files. The latter records also have information about family sizes, health, and income levels. Information about the degree of owner occupancy appears in the block-data maps. There are relatively few records of the names of inhabitants of dwellings. The Pennsylvania direct tax lists show the names of owners and/or occupants, and the sample rent enforcement case files among the records of the Office of the Housing Expediter show the names of tenants and their landlords.

Economic information about housing appears in a variety of record groups. The direct tax lists present the valuation placed on the dwellings. The United States Housing Corporation records reflect the costs of the homes that it constructed and the prices that the homes sold for during the period 1919–29. The District of Columbia Rent Commission files contain information obtained from tenants, landlords, and others regarding rents, original costs of construction, and replacement costs. In the files of PHA we find information regarding the financing of the PWA housing projects and the value and acquisition of the project sites.

The records of the Federal Home Loan Bank System include the so-called city survey files of the Home Owners Loan Corporation, a predecessor agency; these files reflect for some 239 cities, each in excess of 40,000 population, the state of their real estate and mortgage markets during 1935–39. The data are contained in a variety of forms, questionnaires, maps, and transcripts of interviews. The same record group contains a sample of loan-related correspondence in the period 1933–36. Information about the cost of defense housing during the early period of World War II is given in correspondence and audit reports in the HUD record group. The same group has files of the National Voluntary Mortgage Credit Extension Committee for the period 1954–65 that relate to the problems of obtaining mortgages in small towns and rural areas.

As may be expected, the FHA records are a prime source of information about insurance of housing. There are samples of insurance case files for both rental projects and homes, covering the periods 1936–46 and 1934–48, respectively. Both the FHA and the PHA record groups contain data regarding the relative safety—that is economic safety—of insuring housing in various cities during 1937–42 and 1933–39, respectively. Four record groups reflect rentals during distinct periods. The BLS questionnaires have information not only on prime rents but also on the rents paid by boarders of the low-income immigrant residences. The Shipping Board records disclose the rental and sales prices of its emergency housing during World War I.

The best of the rental data are probably in the large-scale block-data maps of 1934–39; this information on average monthly rents in many cities is among the FHA records that derive from the 1934–39 property surveys. There are sample selected rent enforcement case files for the long period from the beginning of United States entry into World War II through the close of the Korean War. Incidentally, there is also information about rentals among the general rent records of the Office of Price Administration in the Office of the Housing Expediter record group.

The records under review are those of the federal government, and they necessarily largely relate to the actual housing programs of its agencies. If we take these chronologically, we find substantial project files and project histories for the emergency housing of World War I in records of the United States Housing Corporation and the United States Shipping Board. Apart from statistical and narrative data about these projects, there is information relating to the relations of these agencies with municipalities. In the 1930s several agencies were concerned with housing. The records of the Office of the Secretary of the Interior for 1933–39, describe the overall administration of housing projects. The minutes of the Reconstruction Finance Corporation for 1935–48 have information about the RFC's role in granting mortgage loans. The correspondence between 1938 and 1954 of the Federal

National Mortgage Association pertains largely to the subject of loans and mortgages.

The PHA records are of several varieties. One of the principal collections is the file relating to projects initiated under the RFC and the PWA during the 1930s. Much of the data in these files about local housing already existent in the areas have been mentioned previously, but the files are also notable for the fact that they relate not only to the approximately sixty completed projects but also to the many more—perhaps more than ten times as many—proposed projects that were not approved. The two series of project files, which in the aggregate extend to 234 linear feet, pertain to about 235 communities; and they contain, apart from the data already reported, information about the health, taxes, and incidence of crime in the urban neighborhoods under review.

With the advent of World War II the PHA was involved in the conversion of private buildings leased to the government to workers' dwellings; there are program files for this. Among other information in PHA files is the manner of selection of local housing personnel, architects, advisory committees, and others associated with housing at the operational level. The RFC records include case files for the Defense Homes program of the years 1900–1948, pertaining to the acquisition of land and construction, maintenance, and disposition of buildings.

The area rent office operations of the Office of the Housing Expediter are documented for the period 1942–51, as are the operations of the Veterans Emergency Housing program in their larger aspects. A general view of the activities of communities in respect to housing during the extreme shortages of the early postwar period is available in the records of the Community Action Advisory Service, a federal body that prodded communities into training workers for housing construction and into acquiring appropriate sites. The locality files of OHE also indicate community action.

A colleague, Mr. William Fraley, has called my attention to the extensive number of petitions, memorials, and letters addressed to congressional committees in connection with the housing legislation of the Great Depression and the early postwar period. These records are bolstered by other records documenting the actual legislative processes that eventuated in acts of Congress. Also indicative of local sentiment about the housing and other New Deal programs are the biweekly and monthly reports to the National Emergency Council that are in the records of the Office of Government Reports for 1934–38.

There are many varieties of data regarding local conditions in the federal records. Taking them chronologically, we find twenty-three linear feet of United States Housing Corporation files of industrial and housing surveys in 1918 that contain questionnaires, reports from local sources, and other records—all having been gathered to determine how adequate were local housing facilities in more than two hundred cities. Correspondence of the Shipping Board from 1917 to 1922 is about local housing facilities, rents, values, and relations with architects and engineers.

Research studies of federal, state, and municipal agencies have been collected in the Work Projects Administration record group; these reflect many local data about housing, including statistics on the distribution of races and of multifamily dwellings. The same record group also contains surveys of housing vacancies from 1937 to 1942. The PHA project files already mentioned have much information about the relations of PWA with private persons and local groups interested in housing. The many submissions by would-be developers, property owners, governments, and others lend great variety to these records. Of particular note is the economic data file of the HUD record groups. These files for 1937–45 reflect factors affecting the supply of and the demand for housing in 412 areas of over 25,000 in population and 1,700 areas of lesser population. Some of the data, it should be added, date from 1850. The same record group contains a series of "Housing Market Analysis" monographs covering 140 metropolitan areas in the period 1939–40 and 120 war industry areas in the period 1941–42.

The Real Property Survey maps of the FHA that were prepared by federal or local authorities during 1934–49 in 362 cities have been mentioned earlier in this paper. But these records and their content are amply and well described in the paper about cartographic records prepared for this conference by Ralph Ehrenberg. Mr. Ehrenberg also has noted the maps, graphs, and tables relating to the growth of cities, sometimes over a period of 200 years. For 1941–45 the records of the Office of Community War Services contain area reports about housing needs, and the HUD files contain monographs on this subject as well as a 5 percent retained sample of files on the same subject for 1942–46 and 1933–35.

Before closing with remarks on the availability of the records, I have several observations. I know that many of the data contained in the federal records have already been summarized and then published or otherwise made available in other forms. Nevertheless, the details remain available in the records for organization in new formats, new groupings, and new tabulations made possible by the computer technology that was not at hand a generation ago. Moreover, the growing interest in small areas (such as neighborhoods) makes details regarding such areas more useful than they would have been regarded in years past. Also, the increasing availability of data on political behavior permits the combination of those with the social data in the housing records.

To what extent are the housing records open for use by researchers? I shall answer this question briefly. The great majority of the housing records are open to research unqualifiedly, and few, if any, are closed unqualifiedly. To say it briefly, those records that are sensitive can be examined upon a permission-of-agency basis. We must consider that there are issues of privacy, trade secrecy, and other characteristics associated with some of these records. Some categories of the data are protected by statutes. Nevertheless, it has been the policy of the National Archives and many federal agencies to grant access to privileged files containing economic and other data given in confidence provided that the researcher agrees to make no disclosure regarding the identity of parties and to compose his published product in such a way that identities cannot be inferred.

PANEL ON
TRANSPORTATION

Urban Mass Transit History: Where We Have Been and Where We Are Going

GLEN E. HOLT

Urban mass transit innovation did not begin in this country until the late 1820s.[1] First came the crude, lumbering omnibus or urban stagecoach, but within a decade the horse railway proved its superiority as a carrying form. The third step came as men applied mechanical power—first steam, then cables, and finally electricity—to urban passenger transport. The final dimension was added when electric cars were run upon elevated structures or underground in subways as forms of rapid transit.[2] Through three-quarters of the nineteenth century these successive innovations facilitated urban development. Collectively they were a primary technological factor which shaped the modern city physically and socially, carrying it from the preindustrial walking city into the age of the metropolis.

Nineteenth-century city dwellers built the streetcar into their daily lives, but they were never satisfied with its performance. In pamphlets, broadsides, and newspaper letter columns they demanded that government officials legislate to secure regular and dependable service from the "necessary nuisance." The introduction of electric traction increased these demands. Urban riders realized the potentials of the innovation, but they perceived that the private corporations were not serving the public in the fullest measure. Those who led the fight for better service believed that a new franchise relationship had to be instituted between the city and the carrying corporations. They insisted that a transit company be regarded "as a contractor for

1. This paper concerns the history of mass transit. For a concise, planning-oriented review article on urban transportation, see Harold M. Mayer, "Cities: Transportation and Internal Circulation," *Journal of Geography* 68 (October 1969): 390–405.

2. The term rapid transit is used in this paper to designate subways and elevateds. Historically, the meaning is not as precise. The most inclusive illustration of its more comprehensive meaning is in Beckles Willson, *The Story of Rapid Transit* (New York: D. Appleton & Co., 1903), in which rapid transit is an umbrella term designating all the technological devices which men had innovated to overcome distance.

the performance of a public service, rather than as a private holder of privileges entitled to exploit a business for unlimited profits."[3]

Those who attempted to discipline the street railway corporations found they had a difficult task. Sometimes they discovered that collusion between legislative agencies and those to be regulated was the basic factor in poor service.[4] Just as frequently, however, they found their own understanding inadequate to form realistic operating standards or to provide guidelines for improved performance. Whether it was the motivation from an exposé of corruption or simply inadequate service, in the last decade of the nineteenth century, a fact-oriented generation set out to explore the nature of its local carrying corporations.[5]

Specially appointed state and local commissions were designated to inquire into transportation questions in cities large and small. The model report which came out of such investigations was produced in 1898 by the Massachusetts legislature's Special Committee on Street Railroads. Chaired by Charles Francis Adams, the Massachusetts team summarized the financial arrangements and the operating and service conditions in fourteen American and seventeen European cities.[6] Adding to the numerous commission publications were reports made by new professional "transportation experts," whose treatises began to appear in the same decade. Men like Bion Arnold, Delos Wilcox, and Frederic Doolittle added a new dimension to an industry which until then had been manned mostly by self-taught engineers and financial speculators. Commissions and experts most frequently studied the largest cities, but together they reported on about one hundred different American communities between the late 1880s and the mid-1920s.[7] Con-

3. Delos F. Wilcox, *Municipal Franchises: A Description of the Terms and Conditions upon Which Private Corporations Enjoy Special Privileges in the Streets of American Cities*, 2 vols. (New York: Engineering News Publishing Co., 1911), 2:6.

4. For accounts of transit corruption, see Lincoln Steffens, *Shame of the Cities* (New York: McClure Phillips & Co., 1904); Edward Bemis, ed., *Municipal Monopolies: A Collection of Papers by American Economists and Specialists* (New York: Thomas Y. Crowell & Co., 1899); William Bennett Munro, *Municipal Government and Administration*, 2 vols. (New York: Macmillan Co., 1923). Each local transit fight produced its own literature of exposé. For St. Louis, see Julius Ceasar Jackson, *United Railways Company's Referendum Burglary* (St. Louis: J. C. Jackson, 1919); and Frank G. Tyrrell, *Political Thuggery; or, Bribery a National Issue. Missouri's Battle with the Boodlers, Including The Great Fight Led by Hon. Joseph W. Folk, Circuit Attorney of St. Louis, and the Uprising of the People of the State* (St. Louis: Puritan Publishing Co., 1904).

5. Robert H. Bremner, *From the Depths: The Discovery of Poverty in the United States* (New York: New York University Press, 1956). Chap. 9 points out this investigative orientation.

6. Massachusetts, Commonwealth of, Special Committee. *Report of Committee Appointed to Investigate the Relations between Cities and Towns and Street Railway Companies.* Charles Francis Adams, Wm. W. Crapo, E. B. Hayes, and Walter S. Allen, secretary (February 1898).

7. [Boston Elevated Railway Library], *Reference List of Literature on Urban Elec-*

comitantly with these investigations, technical experts in electricity, engineering, and finance prepared the first transit industry textbooks, which delimited standard operating practices and outlined equipment options.[8] Also, three different members of the legal profession compiled massive tomes on street railway law.[9] Frederic W. Speirs, a long-term student of the Phila-

tric Railways Indexed by Cities. Compiled from Reports by Railroad Commissions, Public Service Commissions, Legislative Commissions, Investigating Commissions, Electric Railway Companies, Transportation Experts, and Others with Classified Index (Boston: Boston Elevated Railway Library, June 1927); and its supplement, *Urban and Interurban Electric Railways: A Selected List of General Literature* (Boston: Boston Elevated Railway Library, 1930). See also, Adelaide R. Hasse, *Index of Economic Material in Documents of the States* (Washington, D.C.: Carnegie Institute, 1908–22), which contains many references to state reports under its "Street Railway" category. No listing is complete since many local experts were omitted. For example, George Hooker, "Report to the City Council of Chicago on Local Transportation Development in Great Cities" (typescript; Chicago, February 1, 1904), is not mentioned.

8. Among the numerous textbooks are John P. Brooks, *Handbook of Street-Railroad Location* (New York: J. Wiley & Sons, 1898); Carl Hering, *Recent Progress in Electric Railways* (New York: W. J. Johnston Co., 1892); Irville Augustus May, *Street Railway Accounting, a Manual of Operating Practices for Electric Railways* (New York: The Ronald Press Co., 1917); Edwin W. Houston and A. E. Kennelly, *Electric Street Railways* (New York: McGraw Publishing Co., 1896); Louis Bell, *Power Distribution for Electric Railroads* (New York: Street Railway Publishing Co., 1897); Charles B. Fairchild, *Street Railways: Their Construction, Operation, and Maintenance* (New York: Street Railway Publishing Co., 1892). Later Fairchild also wrote a nontechnical popular textbook addressed to young men who might want to enter the business. See his *Training for the Electric Railway Business* (Philadelphia and London: J. B. Lippincott Co., 1919).

9. Henry J. Booth, *A Treatise on the Law of Street Railways, Embracing Surface, Sub-Surface and Elevated Roads, Whether Operated by Animal Power, Electricity, Cable or Steam Motor* (Philadelphia: T. & J. W. Johnson & Co., 1892); Andrew J. Nellis, *The Law of Street Surface Railroads as Compiled from Statutes and Decisions in the Various States and Territories Showing the Manner of Organizing Corporations to Construct and Operate Street Surface Railroads, the Acquisition of Their Franchises and Property, Their Regulations, etc., by Statute and Municipal Ordinance, Their Rights and Liabilities Both as to Other Users of the Streets and Highways and as to Passengers and Employees* (Albany: Matthew Bender & Co., 1902); Andrew J. Nellis, *Street Railroad Accident Law: A Complete Treatise on the Principles and Rules of Law Applied by the Courts of the States and Territories of the United States and Canada in Determining the Liability of Street Railroads, for Injuries to the Person and Property, by Accidents to Passengers, Employees, and Travelers on the Public Streets and Highways, and on the Pleading and Practice in the Various Jurisdictions in Street Railroad Accident Litigation* (Albany: Matthew Bender & Co., 1904); Andrew J. Nellis, *The Law of Street Railroads: A Complete Treatise on the Law Relating to the Organization of Street Railroads, the Acquisition of Their Franchises and Property, Their Regulation by Statute and Ordinance, Their Operation and Liability for Injuries to the Person and Property of Passengers, Employees, and Travelers and Others on the Public Streets and Highways, Including Also Pleading and Practice,* 2d ed., 2 vols. (Albany: Matthew Bender & Co., 1911); Byron Elliott and William F. Elliott, *A Treatise on the Law of Railroads; Containing a Consideration of the Organization, Statutes, and Powers of Railroad Corporations, and of the Rights and Liabilities Incident to the Location, Construction, and Operation of Railroads; Together with Their Duties, Rights, and Liabilities as Carriers, Including both Street and*

delphia transit, summarized the new perspective which came out of this energetic collecting, compiling, and categorizing. "We have . . . passed the period of sweeping generalizations from imperfect data," he wrote in 1900.[10]

All of these studies, including many of the textbooks, made at least some attempt to set the present into an historical perspective, but the most professional retrospective treatment of transit development was produced by a small group of economist-historians. Led by Frederic W. Speirs and James Blaine Walker, these scholars combed through old newspapers, legislative documents, corporate minutes, and court cases, searching for faulty legislation, potentially corrupt political relationships, and forgotten regulations which might be used to discipline the public carriers.[11] In their book-length monographs, these writers balanced the benefits of mass transit against the underlying realities of its relationship with the city and its people. The history students concluded that the transit men's past entrepreneurial and managerial performance was inadequate, and they decided much of the carrying companies' operation had been at least bad business, if not always illegal. Positive changes in riding and service conditions, the scholars found, had come about only through citizen pressure. Ralph Heilman, in his history of Chicago traction, summarized the historic antagonism between citizens and transit companies when he subtitled his 1908 work *A Study of the Efforts of the Public to Secure Good Service.*[12]

Several of these reform-oriented historical studies were not completed until after 1900. They, therefore, overlapped the first decade and a half of the new century, those fifteen years that urban transportation professionals marked out as the "boom days" of the street railway industry.[13] In this period

Interurban Railways (Indianapolis: Bobbs-Merrill Co., 1897). Of a different nature see, James S. Cummins, comp., *State and Territorial General Statutes Relating to the Use of Streets and Highways by Street Railway, Gas, Water, and Electric Light Companies* (Chicago: H. M. Byllesby & Co., 1905).

10. Frederic W. Speirs, "Regulation of Cost and Quality of Service as Illustrated by Street Railway Companies," in *Corporations and Public Welfare* (Addresses at the Annual Meeting of the American Academy of Political and Social Science, Philadelphia, April 19–20, 1900; New York: American Academy of Political and Social Science, 1900).

11. Frederic W. Speirs, *The Street Railway System of Philadelphia: Its History and Present Condition*, Johns Hopkins University Studies in Historical and Political Science, 15th ser., 3, 4, 5 (Baltimore, March, April, May, 1897); James Blaine Walker, *Fifty Years of Rapid Transit, 1864–1917* (New York: Law Printing Co., 1918); Samuel Wilbur Norton, *Chicago Traction: A History Legislative and Political* (Chicago: n.p., 1907); Harry James Carman, *The Street Surface Railway Franchises of New York City*, Studies in History, Economics and Public Law no. 200 (New York: Columbia University, 1919).

12. Ralph E. Heilman, *Chicago Traction: A Study of the Efforts of the Public to Secure Good Service* (Princeton: American Economic Association, 1908).

13. Charles Rufus Harte, "Boom Days of the Electric Railways," *Transit Journal* 78 (September 15, 1934): 329–31.

the per capita riding habit rose steadily, the mileage of track under electric operation increased rapidly, and an interurban railway network, begun in the previous decade, was completed.[14]

Yet in these prosperous days, the urban transit industry already had growing internal weaknesses which made it vulnerable to competition when it came. Some companies went into heavy debt in order to electrify, carrying with them the paper values inherited from the horsecar and cable period. Others overestimated the passenger increase associated with the new power source and built expensive extensions into marginal traffic areas, relying on rapid population growth to wipe the red from their ledgers. Many city councils, growing more watchful of the public interest, forced the carrying companies into tightly bound legal agreements for street maintenance, bridge building, snow removal, and payment of taxes before allowing them to electrify or open new routes. In sum, if an overcapitalized and overextended transit corporation, bound by such agreements, were to remain solvent, its passenger traffic had to increase rapidly.[15]

The commuting public, meanwhile, financed any scheme and tried every available alternative in an attempt to break away from the crowded transit cars and the discipline imposed on personal life style by the necessity of riding a mass carrying system.[16] Then, in 1908, Henry Ford introduced his cheap automobile.[17] Beginning with a trickle, the small autos were soon flooding the streets. Their potential meaning for street railway men was manifested in a single set of statistics. From 1914 to the beginning of 1919, the number of persons per auto dropped from sixty-two to nineteen, and the number of families per car fell from sixteen to five.[18] The electric railways had a real competitor for the first time in their existence.

If automobile competition were not enough to bring difficult times to local carriers, the inflation, the shortage of materials, and the strikes associated

14. U.S., Department of Commerce, Bureau of the Census, *Census of Electrical Industries: Electric Railways and Motor-Bus Operation of Affiliates and Successors, 1932* (Washington, D.C.: Government Printing Office, 1934), pp. 4, 7, 18.

15. Glen E. Holt, "The Changing Perception of Urban Pathology: An Essay on the History of Mass Transit," in Kenneth T. Jackson and Stanley K. Schultz, *Urban America: The Historical Perspective* (New York: Alfred A. Knopf, 1970).

16. The rapid acceptance of the bicycle was one illustration. See Clarence P. Hornung, *Wheels across America* (New York: A. S. Barnes & Co., 1959), pp. 220–67.

17. For the history of the automobile see, John B. Rae, *The American Automobile: A Brief History* (Chicago: University of Chicago Press, 1965); E. D. Kennedy, *The Automobile Industry: The Coming of Age of Capitalism's Favorite Child* (New York: Reynal & Hitchcock, 1941); Frank Donovan, *Wheels for a Nation* (New York: Thomas Y. Crowell Co., 1965).

18. Ralph C. Epstein, *The Automobile Industry: Its Economic and Commercial Development* (Chicago and New York: A. W. Shaw Co., 1928), pp. 317, 340, 344, has tables of statistics on the number of automobile registrations and, after 1903, production figures of low-priced cars.

with World War I added to their operating burdens. At the Federal Electric Railway Commission hearings in the summer of 1919, witnesses generally agreed that the country's urban transportation business had devolved into a state of crisis. Roger W. Babson, an investment broker who had been buying and selling transit stocks for years, summed up the industry's situation when he stated that if Henry Ford "had only been bright enough to sell street railway securities short when he built his plant, he would have been making double the money he is now." Babson went on to tell the commission that no one but anonymous losers like "your Uncle Dudley" and municipalities were investing in the carrying industry.[19] And since there were not enough "Uncle Dudleys" to keep mass transit systems in operation, the public treasury increasingly would have to provide the necessary revenue.

The overall industry response to the challenges of wartime and the decade after was a flurry of innovation and reorganization: many carriers adopted light-weight, one-man cars; others began operating buses; routes were rearranged to provide increased speed and additional service; and, finally, a public relations campaign was launched to popularize and sell mass transportation.[20] But all this frenetic activity had little effect. The 1927 census of the industry showed that the number of revenue passengers had decreased half a billion per year from 1922. When the result of the 1932 census was announced, the scale of the industry's decline was fully revealed. The total number of revenue passengers per year had dropped from twelve billion to eight billion, and in urban areas the average number of trips per capita had gone from 232 to 131.[21] This passenger decrease alone was enough to inspire new examinations of the history of the industry. But at the end of the decade, the decline was associated with deteriorating national economic trends which provided additional incentive for introspection and retrospection over "the transportation crisis."[22]

The cities were hit hard when the depression struck in 1929. Many of the

19. *Proceedings of the Federal Electric Railway Commission*, held in Washington, D.C., during the Months of July, August, September, and October 1919. (Washington, D.C.: Government Printing Office, 1920), p. 1054.

20. Henry H. Norris, ed., *Popularizing Public Transportation*, a digest of presentations made by Electric Railways, August 1, 1927, to the Charles A. Coffin Foundation, *Electric Railway Practices*, 5th ser. (New York: American Electric Railway Association, 1928). The first of these volumes was published as *Electric Railway Practices in 1923*. The first change in title was to *Making Transportation Pay, 1926*; the year following it became *Popularizing Public Transportation*. Then, after skipping a year, a final volume appeared entitled *Selling Transportation*. The volume titles offer an excellent summary of the changing attitude within the industry.

21. Bureau of the Census, *Census of Electrical Industries*, pp. 7, 18: William D. Middleton, *The Time of the Trolley* (Milwaukee: Kalmbach Publishing Co., 1967), pp. 122–24.

22. G. Lloyd Wilson, *The Transportation Crisis* (New York: Sears Publishing Co., 1933), is a very useful general overview. For street railways, see chaps. 12 and 13.

plans for civic improvement, including those for transportation, were laid aside as attention was turned to more pressing social and economic problems. With the city suffering so greatly, scholars were bound to probe the workings of urban institutions, and countless writers produced an abundance of scholarly inquiry on urban themes. Associated with this proliferation, the 1930s was the most productive decade for monographic study of urban transportation history until the 1960s.[23]

One frequent topic of urban analysis during the depression decade was the question of city size, and many scholars pointed out that controlled growth within a planned spatial arrangement might have avoided the inefficiencies and waste which appeared all too apparent in a decade pressed for resources. With this kind of concern, the process of city growth came in for much attention. At the turn of the century Richard Hurd had observed that cities spread out from their center along transportation lines, resulting in a star shape.[24] In the 1930s, three new books expanded on this transit–city-shape relationship.[25] The most important was by Homer Hoyt, who provided a succinct portrayal of the dynamic process by which cities expanded. On the basis of his 142-city study, Hoyt concluded that "high grade residential areas tend[ed] to develop along the fastest existing transportation line," and that the related growth pattern took the form of wedge-shaped sectors which radiated outward from the city's center. This dynamic model thus combined urban transit with the successive movement of residential neighborhoods and shifts in land uses to explain the form of city growth.[26]

Hoyt examined transit development in relationship to the historic real estate bidding process that shaped the city. Other students were concerned

23. For a concise overview of the 1920s and 1930s, including some of the major literature, see, Blake McKelvey, *The Emergence of Metropolitan America, 1915–1966* (New Brunswick, N.J.: Rutgers University Press, 1968), chaps. 2 and 3.

24. Richard M. Hurd, *Principles of City Land Values* (New York: Record & Guide, 1903).

25. Homer Hoyt, *The Structure and Growth of Residential Neighborhoods in American Cities*, U.S. Federal Housing Administration (Washington, D.C.: Government Printing Office, 1939). Hoyt had previously related transportation and land values in his *100 Years of Land Values in Chicago* (Chicago: University of Chicago Press, 1933). Edwin H. Spengler, *Land Values in New York in Relation to Transit Facilities*, Columbia University Studies in History, Economics and Public Law, no. 333 (New York, 1930), had previously found that transit lines acted as facilitators to the emergence of higher land values if an area were desirable in other ways.

26. Intentionally I have not spent time reviewing the other theoretical models of city shape which are less directly concerned with transit development. Three recent books provide brief summaries of all of these models. See Ralph Thomlinson, *Urban Structure: The Social and Spatial Character of Cities* (New York: Random House, 1969), chap. 8; Raymond E. Murphy, *The American City: An Urban Geography* (New York: McGraw-Hill Book Co. 1966), chap. 12; Robert E. Dickinson, *City and Region: A Geographical Interpretation* (London: Routledge & Kegan Paul, 1964), chap. 5.

with the performance of local passenger carriers in a revised political setting. In 1912, Seattle became the first city to own an urban transit system, and in 1929, Harry Leslie Purdy probed the Seattle operation in the first monograph which dealt historically with the municipal management of a transit system.[27] Purdy's main purpose was to judge the quality of performance under public ownership. His conclusion was a qualified endorsement of the effort, although local political interference and a declining passenger trend had acted together to force the Seattle system into deficit operations.[28]

The work of state public service commissions, as it related to mass transit, also came in for attention. Like public ownership, the commissions had their impetus in the 1890s, although none was empowered until the next decade.[29] From the time the regulatory agencies were established, urban transit men complained that state direction was too forceful, cutting their flexibility of operation at a time when they were attempting to meet automobile competition and declining ridership. In the late 1920s and the decade following, several public utilities textbooks included retrospective sections assessing the quality of performance of both the state agencies and the utilities after the commissions had been created. These studies belied the claims of the local carriers. The scholars generally agreed that the transit companies had performed more consistently and at higher standards since being regulated as public utilities than they had when operating as private holders of exclusive privilege.[30]

27. Harry Leslie Purdy, *The Cost of Municipal Operation of the Seattle Street Railway*, University of Washington Publications in the Social Sciences, vol. 8 (Seattle, 1929).

28. Part of the Seattle problem was that the municipality had paid too much for the street railways. See Paul Douglas, "The Seattle Municipal Street Railway System," *Journal of Political Economy* 29 (June 1921): 455–77; Graeme O'Geran, *A History of the Detroit Street Railways* (Detroit: Conover Press, 1931), provides an interpretation of both the fight for municipal operation and briefer coverage of how it worked. On the transit industry's attitude to public ownership in this period, see American Electric Railway Association, Committee on Rapid Transit, *Economics of Rapid Transit* (New York: American Electric Railway Association, 1927), a study presenting the findings of a special committee of the American Electric Railway Association on the subject of transportation in metropolitan areas.

29. The impetus for regulation varied from state to state. In New York the issue was gas; in Wisconsin, the necessity of regulating the operation of both steam and electric railroads. For a summary of thinking which went into creating both the regulating bodies and arguments for public ownership, see "Control of Municipal Public Service Corporations," *Annals of the American Academy of Political and Social Science* 31 (May 1908); and, "Municipal Ownership and Municipal Franchises," *Annals of the American Academy of Political and Social Science* 27 (January 1906).

30. William E. Mosher and Finla G. Crawford, *Public Utility Regulation* (New York: Harper & Brothers, 1933); Martin G. Glaeser, *Outlines of Public Utility Economics* (New York: Macmillan Co., 1927); C. O. Ruggles, *Problems in Public Utility Economics and Management* (New York: McGraw-Hill Book Co., 1933); I. R. Barnes, *Public Utility Control in Massachusetts: A Study in the Commission Regula-*

In 1932, economist Edward S. Mason discussed both public ownership and commission regulation in his *Street Railways of Massachusetts*. Mason's sophisticated monograph picked up the Bay State's transit story in 1890 to analyze what he termed in his subtitle *The Rise and Decline of an Industry*.[31] The electrification of street railways, he wrote, was accomplished before its maintenance and depreciation factors were clearly understood. And when the carriers realized that passengers were not paying the full cost of service, they remained optimistic that rising traffic eventually would balance their deficits. Automobile competition destroyed this possibility, and regulatory agencies were unresponsive when the carriers requested higher fares. Increasingly, the public treasury was the only source large enough to defray the deficit of continued operation. Mason closed his work with as many questions as he answered. His inquiries outlined the major developments in public transportation history for the next four decades:

> A substitute common carrier stands ready to take . . . [the street railway's] place, the motor bus. But is this a complete or only a partial substitute? Can it operate more cheaply, and, if so, under what conditions and with what density of traffic? If the use of the private motor car continues to increase, must not any common carrier increase its charge for service in order to exist? What charge is the public ultimately willing to pay for transportation? If the private motor car is used for the major part of its urban transportation by all except the poorer classes, can the cost of common carriage be paid by the rider?[32]

Five years after Mason's work appeared, Emerson P. Schmidt published his *Industrial Relations in Urban Transportation*.[33] His subject mirrored the increase in scholarly attention given to labor history during the depression decade. Schmidt's major theme was familiar to every labor historian

tion of Security Issues and Rates, Yale Publications in Economics, Social Science and Government, no. 2 (New Haven, 1930); Emery Troxel, *Economics of Public Utilities* (New York: Rinehart & Co., 1947). For additional case studies and a summary of the legal situation in which the commissions operated in the early 1920s when all forty-eight states had commissions, see Delos F. Wilcox, *Depreciation in Public Utilities: Relation of Accrued Depreciation to Annual Depreciation and Maintenance*, National Municipal League Monograph Series (New York, 1925); and *Public Utility Laws: A Summary of the Laws Creating the State Public Utility Commissions, Giving an Analytical Digest of Their Jurisdiction and Powers over Transportation Companies* (New York: American Electric Railway Association, June 1, 1922).

31. Edward S. Mason, *The Street Railway in Massachusetts: The Rise and Decline of an Industry*, Harvard Economic Studies, vol. 37 (Cambridge, 1932).

32. Ibid., pp. 186–87.

33. Emerson P. Schmidt, *Industrial Relations in Urban Transportation* (Minneapolis: University of Minnesota Press, 1937).

who examined the union organizing efforts of a semiskilled or unskilled working group. His narrative carried the laborers from their preliminary local bouts with management over inhuman working conditions, through the amalgamation of local unions, to benefits and pensions in the twentieth century. He concluded that urban transportation workers had faced a management more backward than that of most industries and had organized only in the face of extreme adversity.[34]

Schmidt's book is more than the labor history of a single industry, however. The words of his preface mark the singular significance of this volume in the literature of mass transit history. "A thorough search of many libraries and bibliographical sources has revealed no account of the rise and development of urban transportation in the United States," he wrote. "The present volume is designed to fill this gap." The first half of Schmidt's monograph is dedicated to correcting this research hiatus, and his book marks the first attempt to provide a general history of mass transit in the United States.[35]

Within half a decade after Schmidt's work appeared, a second attempt was made to provide an overall history of the mass passenger carrying industry. In 1941, John Anderson Miller brought out his *Fares Please!*[36] In the presagement of a major theme of transit history in the 1950s, Miller concentrated on the nostalgic "romance" and "the presence of many vivid

34. Earlier documents and articles paved the way for Schmidt's work. See especially, *Wage History of the Amalgamated Association of Street and Electric Railway Employees of America, November 1, 1914* (Detroit: W. D. Mahon, International President, 1914); U.S., Department of Labor, Bureau of Labor Statistics, *Street Railway Employment in the United States,* Bulletin of the United States Bureau of Labor Statistics, no. 204 (Washington, D.C.: Government Printing Office, April 1917); B. M. Squires, "Women Street Railway Employees," *Monthly Labor Review* 6 (May 1918); *Analysis of Electric Railway Operating Costs and the Cost of Living, As Related to Wages of Conductors, Motormen, and Other Train Men, Part I* (Prepared under Supervision and Presented by Arthur Sturgis; n.p.: Amalgamated Association of Street and Electric Railway Employees of America, probably 1919); *Cost of Living Studies, IV. Spending Ways of a Semi-Skilled Group: A Study of the Incomes and Expenditures of Ninety-eight Street-Car Men's Families in the San Francisco East Bay Region,* comp. under the direction of the Heller Committee for Research in Social Economics of the University of California; University of California Publications in Economics, vol. 5, no. 5 (Berkeley, March 20, 1931), pp. 295–366. After Schmidt's book appeared, two other treatments, one brief and one book-length, appeared. See H. Dewey Anderson and Percy E. Davidson, *Occupational Trends in the United States* (Stanford, Calif.: Stanford University Press, 1940), pp. 398–402; and, James J. McGinley, *Labor Relations in the New York Rapid Transit Systems, 1904–1944* (New York: King's Crown Press, Columbia University, 1949).

35. After Mason and Schmidt, textbook writers, citing their works, added small sections on street railways. See, for example, Kent T. Healy, *The Economics of Transportation in America: The Dynamic Forces in Development, Organization, Functioning, and Regulation* (New York: Ronald Press, 1940), especially pp. 18–19, 22, 30.

36. John Anderson Miller, *Fares Please! From Horse Cars to Streamliners* (New York: D. Appleton-Century Co. 1941).

personalities" in the industry's development. Meanwhile, he provided an insider's view of the major technological innovations from omnibus to motorbus. Miller's book gave heavy emphasis to the industry's achievements. Less well explained were transit's relation to urban development, the evolution of a regulatory framework, and the shifts which had occurred in finance and ownership. His book was a colorful narrative told by a man who loved his subject, but it was mainly a topical overview, and it lacked analytical depth.[37]

Rationing forced people to ride mass transit during World War II, and passenger figures, which had been declining since the mid-1920s, jumped to their greatest peak in 1946, when over nineteen billion people rode public transit. But with postwar prosperity, the transit-riding trend swung down once more, and patronage declined by over 64 percent from 1945 to 1966. Meanwhile the ratio of operating expense to revenues rose from 77 percent to over 96 percent in the same period. Buses, put on American streets before World War I, became the only form of transit in all but the largest urban areas.[38] Many cities spent money on planning rapid transit schemes. But there was more talk than action, as the realities of inflated construction costs, the long period of time before completion, and political differences among the various units of the balkanized metropolis all hampered building efforts. The federal government meanwhile, after 1944, began to pay part of the cost of urban highway construction, but until 1961 no federal funds were available to complete mass transit schemes. By 1970, the casual rider and the transportation expert shared the perception of an urban transit industry in limbo—without strength for a rebirth but kept alive by hope for the future and occasional doles from the public purse.[39]

37. William Fullerton Reeves, *The First Elevated Railroads in Manhattan and the Bronx of the City of New York* (New York: New York Historical Society, 1936), is comparable in quality and style, although on a narrower subject.

38. Bus history has not received much attention. The only recent volume of scholarly significance is Burton B. Crandall, *The Growth of the Intercity Bus Industry* (Syracuse, N.Y.: n.p., 1954). This book is concerned primarily with the bus as an intercity carrier as is most of the other literature. Urban operation is covered to some extent in one way or another in all of the following: Percival White, *Motor Transportation of Merchandise and Passengers* (New York: McGraw-Hill Book Co., 1923); Roy Hauer and George H. Scragg, *Bus Operating Practice* (New York: International Motor Co., 1925); Christopher T. Brunner, *The Problem of Motor Transport: An Economic Analysis* (London: Ernest Bean, 1928); Ping Nan Wang, *Rail and Motor Carriers: Competition and Regulation* (Philadelphia: University of Pennsylvania Press, 1932); Malcolm M. Willey and Stuart A. Rice, *Communications Agencies and Social Life* (New York: McGraw-Hill Book Co., 1933); Lewis C. Sorrell, *Passenger Transport in the United States, 1920–1950* (Chicago: Railway Business Association, January 1942). The first issue of the bus industry's journal, *Bus Transportation*, appeared in 1922. It is useful, not only for motor carrier history, but for an examination of electric transit–bus competition.

39. Useful overviews of the postwar transit crisis are found in *Urban Mass Trans-*

Signaling the post–World War II demise of electric street railways, a new group of historians set out to capture the nostalgia and color of that defunct section of the mass transit industry. These students treated history as an avocation. Sometimes their interest was local history, more frequently they were "trolley fans," the name of one of their publications which certainly describes them. In their earliest years, they devoted their attention almost entirely to the "nuts and bolts" of electric traction, and their passion for detail was excelled only by the encyclopedic city historians of the late nineteenth and early twentieth century. Within the last half decade, much of the trolley fans' history has become more sophisticated. Some of their publications relate transit development to urban growth with maps and statistics, analyze past entrepreneurial decisions, and provide general historical accounts which include intercity comparisons of transit development. As we enter a new decade, these nonprofessional historians continue to be the major producers of mass transit history (see Appendix A to this paper for a list of publications).

Paralleling the postwar historical interest of the trolley fans, a development within the history profession provided new incentive to the study of intracity transportation. American urban history was pioneered as a field of special study in the 1930s and 1940s, but it was not until the next decade that it began to be studied widely. After that the growth of the field was rapid, reflecting the concern of citizens and scholars alike over the newest "urban crisis" (see Appendix B for an extensive bibliography).

Urban transportation received its share of attention from those postwar scholars who studied the history of the city. Their research concern was not for the industry, itself, however, but with the carrying agents' relationship to city form and the urbanization process. Sam Warner's 1962 study of Boston's *Streetcar Suburbs* was the landmark monograph in this area.[40] He wrote that mass transit was one of the "large institutions" which shaped the process of residential location. The carrying innovations were the technological mechanism which transformed Boston from a walking city into a metropolis. In the process, thousands of individual home buyers exercised their bidding power in the free real estate market. The resulting residential segregation of different social classes reflected the quality of streetcar service.

portation in Perspective (New York: Tax Foundation, 1968); Wilfred Owen, *Cities in the Motor Age* (New York: Viking Press, 1959); Wilfred Owen, *The Metropolitan Transportation Problem* (Garden City, N.Y.: Doubleday & Co., 1956). More recently, George M. Smerk, *Readings in Urban Transportation* (Bloomington: Indiana University Press, 1968), provides an excellent collection of basic documents and readings.

40. Sam B. Warner, Jr., *Streetcar Suburbs: The Process of Growth in Boston, 1870–1900* (Cambridge: Harvard University Press and M.I.T. Press, 1962). Warner elaborated on the residential segregation theme in his *The Private City: Philadelphia in Three Periods of Its Growth* (Philadelphia: University of Pennsylvania Press, 1968).

Warner's study included the effects of omnibus and horse railway as well as electric transit. Other students also began examining these earlier innovations, setting them into a broad urban perspective and detailing their relationship to city growth. George Rogers Taylor led the way. Turning his research talents away from intercity transportation, he re-created in a lengthy article the story of how the omnibus, horse railway, the steam railroad served the urbanites of Philadelphia, Boston, and New York between 1820 and 1860.[41] Meanwhile, Charles J. Kennedy examined steam railroad commuter service in the Boston area between 1835 and 1860, and Harold E. Cox probed social issues involved in Philadelphia's early transport.[42]

Other topics as well received historical treatment. Arthur Krim, in a unique and outstanding study, explained the timing of mass transit adoption as a function of urban growth and diffusion of information through a city system.[43] The transit–real estate market–city growth relationship was explored by three different scholars.[44] The recent decline in suburban railway commuting was detailed by another.[45] Biography, too, was part of the transit history picture. A long article provided a "portrait of a robber baron" in a sketch of traction entrepreneur Charles T. Yerkes, and a book-length study of *The Man Who Ran the Subways* examined the career of union boss, Mike Quill.[46] The interurban network received exhaustive coverage in one study and was treated summarily in another.[47] Denver's cable railways,

41. George Rogers Taylor, "The Beginnings of Mass Transportation in Urban America," *Smithsonian Journal of History* 1 (Summer and Autumn 1966): 35–50, 31–54.

42. Charles J. Kennedy, "Commuter Services in the Boston Area, 1835–1860," *Business History Review* 36 (Summer 1962): 153–70; Harold E. Cox, "Jim Crow in the City of Brotherly Love: The Segregation of Philadelphia Horse Cars," *Negro History Bulletin* 26 (1962): 119–23; Harold E. Cox, " 'Daily Except Sunday': Blue Laws and the Operation of Philadelphia Horsecars," *Business History Review* 39 (September 1965): 228–42.

43. Arthur Krim, "The Innovation and Diffusion of the Street Railway in North America" (Master's thesis, Department of Geography, University of Chicago, 1967).

44. Jerome D. Fellman, "Pre-Building Growth Patterns of Chicago," *Annals of the Association of American Geographers* 47 (March 1957): 59–82; George M. Smerk, "The Streetcar: Shaper of American Cities," *Traffic Quarterly* 21 (October 1967): 569–84; James Leslie Davis, *The Elevated System and the Growth of Chicago*, Northwestern University Studies in Geography, no. 10 (Evanston, 1965); see also, Harlan W. Gilmore, *Transportation and the Growth of Cities* (Glencoe, Ill.: Free Press, 1953), pp. 108–20.

45. George W. Hilton, "The Decline of Railroad Commutation," *Business History Review* 36 (Summer 1962): 171–87.

46. Sidney I. Roberts, "Portrait of a Robber Baron: Charles T. Yerkes," *Business History Review* 35 (Autumn 1961): 344–71; L. H. Whittemore, *The Man Who Ran the Subways: The Story of Mike Quill* (New York: Holt, Rinehart & Winston, 1968).

47. George W. Hilton and John F. Due, *The Electric Interurban Railways in America* (Stanford, Calif.: Stanford University Press, 1960); Mildred M. Walmsley, "The Bygone Electric Interurban Railway System," *Professional Geographer* 17 (1965): 1–6. See also, Harold Barger, *The Transportation Industries, 1889–1946: A Study of*

Cincinnati's steam cars, and the Pomona, California, streetcars all were treated briefly.[48] More importantly, comparative historical studies of British and American cities began to occur and more appeared likely.[49] And, finally, a Harvard librarian provided the first modern compilation of the sources for the study of street railway history.[50]

This summary has shown us where we have been in the history of urban mass transportation. My survey has revealed that it is a field in which scholars from many disciplines have worked, more often than not with the purpose of seeking a usable past to provide insight, understanding, and sometimes a basis for action for those living in the present. The survey reveals too that much of the historical literature is as concerned with other themes as it is with a transportation topic. This fact has led to both a rich reward and a problem. The reward is the fascinating variety in the historical literature, with its many different concerns and its numerous methodologies.[51] The problem is that the history has been fragmentary, and more remains unknown than concluded on nearly every topic. Everything cannot be studied at once, however, so the next question must be—where should we go from here?

First, transportation historians would do well to break transit history from its localistic mold.[52] Most basically, comparative study is needed. In most

Output, Employment, and Productivity (New York: National Bureau of Economic Research, 1951). In addition, a company history of a large interurban system has been completed recently. See William Smith McDonald, "The Union Traction Company of Indiana " (Ph.D. diss., Department of Geography, Ball State University, 1969).

48. George W. Hilton, "Denver's Cable Railways," *Colorado Magazine* 44 (Winter 1967): 35–52; John H. White, Jr., "By Steam Car to Mt. Lookout: The Columbia and Cincinnati Street Railroad," *Bulletin of the Cincinnati Historical Society* 25 (April 1967): 93–107; Dennis Aronson, "The Pomona Street Railways in the Southern California Boom of the 1880's," *Southern California Quarterly* 47 (September 1965): 245–68.

49. See especially, David Ward, "A Comparative Historical Geography of Streetcar Suburbs in Boston, Massachusetts, and Leeds, England: 1850–1920," *Annals of the Association of American Geographers* 54 (1964): 477–89; David Neft, "Some Aspects of Rail Commuting: New York, London, and Paris," *Geographical Review* 49 (1959): 151–63. British historians have been doing excellent work on urban transport history which is very useful for comparison. See P. A. Keen, "Metropolitan Railway Road Services," *Journal of Transport History* 1 (November 1954): 216–37; G. C. Dickinson, "The Development of Suburban Road Passenger Transport in Leeds, 1840–95," *Journal of Transport History* 4 (November 1960): 214–23; T. C. Barker, "Passenger Transport in Nineteenth Century London," *Journal of Transport History* 6 (May 1964): 166–74.

50. Foster Palmer, "The Literature of the Street Railways," *Harvard Library Bulletin* 12 (Winter 1958): 117–38.

51. See Robert Allen Skotheim, *The Historian and the Climate of Opinion* (Reading, Mass.: Addison-Wesley Publishing Co., 1969), for a review of how American history generally has shifted its emphasis during the twentieth century.

52. Trolley fans' research could be of more significance in comparative investigation than it is. Michael Robbins offers some suggestions in the context of British loco-

cases, however, the foundation for such study has not yet been laid. Comparative studies, therefore, probably should be directed to examining narrowly defined questions with brief time spans. Some potential topics in the period between 1885 and 1920 might include, for example, intermodal competition between street railway, bus and automobile; the nationalization of electric railway financial investments; and the shifts in journey-to-work patterns in different kinds of cities.[53] In more recent decades, the organization of urban and regional transit authorities,[54] the "revolution in transportation planning method,"[55] and different marketing or public selling schemes all have potential as manageable research topics.[56]

Second, historians need to establish transit's historic association with the other technological support mechanisms of the metropolis. Transportation alone did not shape the nineteenth- or twentieth-century city. The availability of adequate water and sewerage systems, ample gas and electric power, and the telephone and, more recently, television, all had an influence on land use, job distribution, and residential location. If we could establish the relationship of this cluster of technological variables, separately and together, as the preindustrial city became a metropolis, we would be much closer to understanding the process of urbanization, a subject which has had too little study by historians.[57]

motive history. See Michael Robbins, "[Review of] *The North Staffordshire Railways* by 'Manifold,'" *Journal of Transport History* 1 (May 1953): 60–61.

53. The financial literature of the street railway industry is reviewed by Palmer, "The Literature." See also as one company example, *Electric Railway and Lighting Properties Managed by Stone and Webster* ([Annual Investor's Handbook]; Boston: Stone & Webster, 1908); Irston F. Barnes, *The Economics of Public Utility Regulation* (New York: F. S. Crofts & Co., 1942), pp. 69–71. Journey-to-work data is available in the various transit studies done in this period. For bibliography, see Boston Elevated Railway Library, *Reference List,* and its supplement.

54. A beginning is found in Robert G. Smith, *Public Authorities, Special Districts, and Local Government* (Washington, D.C.: National Association of Counties, 1964).

55. Mel Scott, *American City Planning since 1890. A History Commemorating the Fiftieth Anniversary of the American Institute of Planners* (Berkeley and Los Angeles: University of California Press, 1969), briefly discusses the shifts in the planning method over the past seventy years. On a more specific change, see Robert B. Mitchell, "Transportation Problems and Their Solution," *Proceedings of the American Philosophical Society* 106 (June 29, 1962): 170–76; Richard M. Zettel and Richard R. Carll, *Summary Review of Major Metropolitan Area Transportation Studies in the United States* (Berkeley: University of California Institute of Transportation and Traffic Engineering, 1962), provide an introduction to the variety of studies which exist.

56. The potential for historical study is suggested by the publication of Lewis M. Schneider, *Marketing Urban Mass Transit: A Comparative Study of Management Strategies* (Boston: Harvard University, Division of Research, Graduate School of Business, 1965).

57. Roy Lubove, "Urbanization, Technology and the Historian" (Paper read in a joint session on Technology and Urbanization, delivered at the Organization of American Historians Convention in 1966, mimeographed.) For a more recent review, see his paper cited in Appendix B. At the same meeting, Sam Warner, in "Transportation

Third, less grand in its conceptualization, but historically significant just the same, the social and political impact which transit innovation exerted on city dwellers needs further work. Nineteenth-century neighborhood leaders considered a public transportation line so beneficial that they organized to lobby for its placement through their areas.[58] But the building of transit lines had social costs as well. British historian H. J. Dyos reports that a minimum of 71,000 people suffered residential displacement because of the entrance of steam railroads into London between 1853 and 1900.[59] Also, the building of some American transit systems brought disruption. A preliminary search of legal records and court cases provides evidence that American urban transportation installations were attacked for everything from destruction of property access to impingement on the sanctity of the bedroom; and court suits became more numerous as the carrying devices grew more powerful.[60] In their eagerness for urban progress, city fathers minimized such claims; and, because the records have not been examined, the social costs of transit innovation remains unexplored except for minor examples.[61]

Fourth, we need research on commuter attitudes about the journey to work. As a preliminary point of departure, I suggest that the public of the 1970s does not perceive the congestion of commuting the same way as urbanites perceived it in 1800 or 1900. In the pretransit city, congestion was primarily the process of people moving about on foot. Mass transit cars reshaped this congestion of mobility. While they allowed many people to live in low-density suburbs, the commuter still had "to endure at least one or two hours a day of most uncomfortable and unhealthful congestion of population in the cars themselves."[62] When people moved out of mass transit cars and into their own automobiles, they removed themselves from both of the older types of congestion. Not only did the automobile provide new freedom in controlling travel times and routing, it also allowed the commuter to pri-

and the City," reviewed the effects of intercity transportation development on the metropolis.

58. As an example of neighborhood competition for horsecars, see *Missouri Republican,* February 9, 1877, p. 8; February 18, 1877, p. 10; Walter B. Stevens, *St. Louis: The Fourth City, 1764–1909,* 3 vols. (St. Louis: S. J. Clarke Publishing Co., 1909), 1:448–52. For a neighborhood effort to secure the Chicago elevated, see John C. Spray, *Book of Woodlawn* (Chicago: John C. Spray, 1920), p. 10.

59. H. J. Dyos, "Some Social Costs of Railway Building in London," *Journal of Transport History* 3 (1957): 24–29.

60. John R. Kellett, "Urban and Transport History from Legal Records: An Example from Glasgow Solicitors' Papers," *Journal of Transport History* 6 (November 1964): 222–37, offers suggestions for British historians, but American historians can find many ideas there.

61. Photographs, especially those taken during construction, may provide initial information about the effect of such devices on a neighborhood. For Chicago, see Harold M. Mayer and Richard C. Wade, with the assistance of Glen E. Holt, *Chicago: Growth of a Metropolis* (Chicago: University of Chicago Press, 1969), p. 211.

62. Wilcox, *Municipal Franchises,* 2:7.

vatize his commuting experience. Within his automobile he avoided the irritating or at least boring contacts with strange people in crowded public places. When the automobile came to dominate traffic, congestion became primarily vehicular. And within his automobile, the commuter faced congestion in a privately controlled setting walled off from the crowd. Commuting, which had been among men's most public daily experiences in the nineteenth century, became one of his most private times in the age of the automobile.[63]

Class and racial differences, too, have been issues in mass transit riding, to the point where they became public controversies and the subject of legislation regulating public carriers. For example, nineteenth-century cities forced workers with muddy boots or those with hand tools to ride on open platforms; the "better sort" of Philadelphia and St. Louis decreed that workers could not have Sunday horsecar outings to the suburbs because the noise of their operation interrupted the hymns and prayers of the faithful in churches along the lines;[64] black men had to conduct the equivalent of a modern sit-in in the 1870s before they were allowed to ride in Louisville; and in the 1860s, in the city of Brotherly Love they had to go to court to obtain the same right.[65] Such fragmentary examples only illustrate the potential of this subject.

The sources with which to do the research I have proposed are adequate though often difficult of access. The base of secondary literature is large, if diffuse in its character. The law, both legislative and judicial, is generally the easiest beginning place, and it offers an exciting potential source which has been much neglected. Comparative statistical sources, too, are available, especially after 1890.[66] Beyond this documentation, however, research is

63. Holt, "Changing Perception."
64. Cox, Daily Except Sunday"; Stevens, *St. Louis,* pp. 439–40; Speirs, "Street Railway System," pp. 18–27.
65. The best volume which shows development of a black ghetto is Gilbert Osofsky, *Harlem: The Making of a Ghetto: Negro New York, 1890–1930* (New York: Harper & Row, 1966). Cox, "Jim Crow," pp. 119–23; Judith Walzer, "Segregation in Louisville, 1867–1890" (Unpublished paper; Chicago, 1966), pp. 24–28. On the racial factor in contemporary transit, see Governor's Commission on the Los Angeles Riots, *Violence in the City: An End or a Beginning, December 2, 1965* (Chairman, John A. McCone); *The Report of the White House Conference "To Fulfill These Rights," June 1–2, 1966* (Washington, D.C., 1966), pp. 32–33; *Report of the National Advisory Commission on Civil Disorders* (A *New York Times* Book; New York: Bantam Books, 1968), pp. 392–93; John F. Kain, "The Big Cities' Big Problem," *Challenge* (September–October 1966), pp. 5–8; J. R. Meyer, J. F. Kain, and M. Wohl, *The Urban Transportation Problem* (Cambridge: Harvard University Press, 1965), pp. 144–67; Oscar A. Ornati, with assistance from James W. Whittaker and Richard Solomon, *Transportation Needs of the Poor: A Case Study of New York City* (New York: Praeger Publishers, 1969); James O. Wheeler, "Transportation Problems in Negro Ghettos," *Sociology and Social Research* 53 (January 1969): 171–79.
66. The Greenwood Press has recently made one source of street railway labor his-

sometimes difficult. The sources for much that is undone in urban transportation history are scattered throughout the nation's cities, often without indexing or cataloging. Much of the basic information remains buried in unindexed newspapers. "Photographs should not be neglected: they can provide evidence, not merely embellishments for a text."[67] So, too, can city maps. Not only do such visual sources provide insights about the nature of a transit operation, but density relationships and corridor development often can be examined more quickly in these sources than in any other way.

My summary has dealt with where we have been and where we are going. To this I have added some directions I believe we should be taking and the availability of sources to reach our destination. The question with which I am left concerns our own time and the future.

Two articles have already appeared which attempt to write the future history of urban transportation. In 1967 James H. Graebner, of the Westinghouse Air Brake Company, provided one prognostication with his article, "Tomorrow's History: Some Pointers from the Past."[68] A year earlier Wilfred Owen assessed present-day developments through the gambit of a mythical "Message from the President of the United States relative to Transportation and the City" dated March 31, 1986.[69] Owen fantasied a Department of Transportation which planned a "balanced approach to urban movement"; the growth of short-haul air transport which, with other forces, acted to bring the development of new, well-organized urbanized regions; and a planned urban policy which sought to reduce the necessity of commuting.

Graebner's article was no fantasy. He dealt with the very real historical constraints which affect the mass transit industry. Political fragmentation of the metropolis; the staggering cost and long lead time necessary to complete a transit plan; the difficulty of recruiting qualified managers; the overemphasis on exotic technological solutions;[70] and the low esteem of mass

tory more accessible with the publication in microfilm of several consecutive years of state labor reports of thirteen states. Most transit statistics still remain locked in the annual reports of state railroad commissions or state public service commissions.

67. Michael Robbins, "What Kind of Railway History Do We Want," *Journal of Transport History* 3 (November 1957): 68. This conceptual article is an excellent beginning for any historian doing work in transportation history.

68. James H. Graebner, "Tomorrow's History: Some Pointers from the Past," *A Report on the Brotherhood of Railroad Trainmen's 1967 Conference on Mass Transportation*, Brotherhood of Railroad Trainmen Mass Transportation Series, vol. 2 (Brotherhood of Railroad Trainmen, 1968).

69. Wilfred Owen, "Transportation and the Cities," *Transportation Journal* 6 (Winter 1966): 24–32.

70. For some examples, see Frank H. Greenwood, "Monorails for Metropolitan Transportation," *Transportation Journal* 3 (Fall 1963): 26–29; Henry S. Reuss, "Research Is Needed to Develop New Modes of Urban Transport," *Transportation Journal* 5 (Winter 1965): 21–26; Henry Fagin, "Urban Mobility and Transportation Technology: Prospects for Relief," *Transportation Journal* 3 (Fall 1963): 20–25; John Fellow, "What's Right (and Wrong) with the Metroliner," *Trains* 29 (July 1969):

carriers in the eyes of the public were all cataloged. Graebner made suggestions that could be used to overcome these restraints, but his article offered no hope that they would be implemented.[71] Whether solutions are found or not, present transit policy will shape the pattern of future transit history. At this moment, it seems likely that historians who write the transit history of the 1960s and 1970s will spend more time chronicling the continuances of urban transport problems than they will in narrating how the transit industry helped solve the ills of the present age.

27–29; William D. Middleton, "Turbotrain Revisited," *Trains* 30 (March 1970): 32–39. On high-speed railroads, see also Sen. Claiborne Pell, *Megalopolis Unbound* (New York: Frederick A. Praeger, 1966).

71. Some literature has appeared which addresses itself to Graebner's concerns. Lewis M. Schneider, *Marketing Urban Mass Transit: A Comparative Study of Management Strategies* (Cambridge: Division of Research, Graduate School of Business Administration, Harvard University, 1965); Robert Don Heidorn, "Urban Mass Transportation with Special Emphasis on Downstate Illinois Cities: A Study in the Formation of Public Policy" (Ph.D. diss., Department of Political Science, University of Illinois, 1963); Elbert Wilham Segelhorst, "Fare Structure of Commuter Railroads and Traffic Congestion in the Central City" (Ph.D. diss., Department of Economics, Columbia University, 1963); Thomas Edward Lisco, "The Value of Commuters' Travel Time: A Study in Urban Transportation" (Ph.D. diss., Department of Geography, University of Chicago, 1967); Michael N. Danielson, *Federal-Metropolitan Politics and the Commuter Crisis* (New York: Columbia University Press, 1965); George M. Smerk, *Urban Transportation: The Federal Role* (Bloomington, Ind.: Indiana University Press, 1965); Joel Smith, *Some Social Aspects of Mass Transit in Selected American Cities* (East Lansing, Mich.: Michigan State University, 1959); Louis K. Lowenstein, *The Location of Residences and Work Places in Urban Areas* (New York: Scarecrow Press, 1965); William R. McGrath, "Urban Transport As an Urban Problem," *Traffic Quarterly* 21 (July 1967): 307–20. A good statement of concrete research needs is *A Key to Change: Urban Transportation Research*, Highway Research Board, Special Report 69 (Presented at the Forty-first Annual Meeting, January 8–12, 1962; Washington, D.C.: National Academy of Sciences-National Research Council, 1962).

APPENDIX A:
PUBLICATIONS ON MASS TRANSIT HISTORY

The trolley fans have their own organizations, including the Electric Railroaders' Association, the Electric Railway Historical Society, and the Central Electric Railfans' Association. Many of these groups publish their own periodicals and pamphlets.

The best general histories are William D. Middleton, *The Time of the Trolley* (Milwaukee: Kalmbach Publishing Co., 1967); and Frank Rowsome, Jr., *Trolley Car Treasury: A Century of American Streetcars, Horsecars, Cable Cars, Interurbans, and Trolleys* (New York: Bonanza Books, 1956). Two general popular histories of transportation also include coverages of mass transportation. See Edward L. Throm, *Popular Mechanics' Picture History of American Transportation* (New York: Simon & Schuster, 1952); and Clarence P. Hornung, *Wheels across America* (New York: A. S. Barnes & Co., 1959). William D. Middleton, *The Interurban Era* (Milwaukee: Kalmbach Publishing Co., 1961) details the operation of the electric railways between cities. For California interurbans, see Spencer Crump, *Ride the Big Red Cars: How Trolleys Helped Build Southern California* (Los Angeles: Crest Publications, 1962).

Typical of the specialized writing on a single city are Stephen A. Kieffer, *Transit and the Twins* (Minneapolis: Twin City Rapid Transit Co., 1958); Richard M. Wagner and Roy J. Wright, *Cincinnati Streetcars* (No. 1, "Horsecars and Steam Dummies"; No. 2, "The Inclines"; Cincinnati: Wagner Car Company, March 1, 1968); Elizabeth Kennerly Russell, "The Narrow-Gauge and Its Patrons," *Bulletin of the Missouri Historical Society* 6 (April 1950): 273–83; Leslie Blanchard, *The Street Railway Era in Seattle: A Chronicle of Six Decades* (Forty Fort, Pa.: Harold E. Cox, 1968); James J. Buckley, *The Evanston Railway Co.*, Bulletin no. 28, Electric Railway Historical Society (February 1958); Berl Katz, *St. Louis Cable Railways*, Bulletin no. 44, Electric Railway Historical Society (February 1965); Louis C. Hennick and E. Harper Charlton, *The Streetcars of New Orleans: Louisiana—Its Street and Interurban Railways*, 2 vols. (Shreveport, La.: Louis C. Hennick, 1965), 2.

Examples of the writing on streetcar technology are Randolph L. Kulp,

100

ed., *History of Lehigh Valley Transit Company* (Allentown, Pa.: Lehigh Valley Chapter, National Railway Historical Society, April 1, 1966); Phil and Mike Palmer, *The Cable Cars of San Francisco* (Berkeley: Howell-North, 1959); James D. Johnson, comp., *A Century of Chicago Streetcars, 1858–1958* (Wheaton, Ill.: Traction Orange Co., 1964); Ian Arnold, *Locomotive, Trolley, and Rail Car Builders: An All-Time Directory* (Los Angeles: Trans-Anglo Books, 1965); Lucius Beebe and Charles Clegg, *Cable Car Carnival* (Oakland, Calif.: Grahame Hardy, 1951).

Recently the trolley fans have also begun to reprint their own primary resources. See, for example:

Thorburn Reid, *Some Early Traction History* (Reprint from *Cassier's Magazine*, August 1899. *Traction Collector's Library*, vol. 2. Montreal: Trains and Trolleys, December 1968).

John A. Brill, The Development of the Streetcar (Reprint from *Cassier's Magazine*, August 1899. *Traction Collector's Library*, vol. 1. Montreal: Trains and Trolleys, December 1968).

Growth of Leading American Electric Railways: United Railways of St. Louis (Reprint from *Brill Magazine*, 1925; Bulletin no. 41, Electric Railway Historical Society).

Cars of the St. Louis Car Company, 1927 (Reprint from St. Louis Car Company's 1927 catalog with two 1928 supplements; Bulletin no. 18, Electric Railway Historical Society).

The Street Railway System of St. Louis (Reprint from *Street Railway Journal*, vol. 11, 1895. *Traction Heritage*, vol. 2. Indianapolis: Vane A. Jones, 1969).

The System of Wire-Cable Railways for Cities and Towns as Operated in San Francisco, Los Angeles, Chicago, St. Louis, Kansas City, New York, Cincinnati, Hoboken, etc. (Reprint from the Pacific Cable Railway Company, San Francisco, 1887, Glenwood Publishers, 1967).

APPENDIX B:
PUBLICATIONS ON URBAN HISTORY

The following list contains references to the basic bibliographic articles, books of readings, and general overviews of urban history.

Briggs, Asa. "The Study of Cities." *Confluence* 7 (1958).

Brooks, Robert C. "A Bibliography of Municipal Problems and City Conditions." *Municipal Affairs* 1 (1897): 1–234; Revised version, *Municipal Affairs* 5 (1901): 1–346.

Callow, Jr., Alexander B., ed. *American Urban History: An Interpretative Reader with Commentaries.* New York: Oxford University Press, 1969.

Coan, Otis W., and Lillard, Richard G. *America in Fiction: An Annotated List of Novels.* 5th ed. Palo Alto, Calif.: Pacific Books, 1967.

Cross, Robert D. *The Church and the City, 1865–1910.* Indianapolis: Bobbs-Merrill Co., 1967.

Daland, R. J. "Political Science and the Study of Urbanism: A Bibliographic Essay." *American Political Science Review* 51 (1957): 491–509.

Davis, Allen F. "The American Historian vs. the City." *Social Studies* 56 (1965): 91–96, 127–35.

Degler, Carl N. "American Political Parties and the Rise of the City: An Interpretation." *Journal of American History* 51 (1964): 41–59.

Diamond, William. "On the Dangers of the Urban Interpretation of History." In *Historiography and Urbanization: Essays in Honor of W. Stull Holt*, edited by Eric Goldman, pp. 67–108. Baltimore: Johns Hopkins Press, 1941.

Gelfant, Blanche H. *The American City Novel.* Norman, Okla.: University of Oklahoma Press, 1954.

Ginger, Ray, ed. *Modern American Cities.* A *New York Times* Book; Chicago: Quadrangle Books, 1969.

Glaab, Charles N. *The American City.* Homewood, Ill.: Dorsey Press, 1963.

———. "The Historian and the American City: A Bibliographic Survey." In Philip M. Hauser and Leo F. Schnore, *The Study of Urbanization.* Chap. 2. New York: John Wiley & Sons, 1965.

———. "The Historian and the American Urban Tradition." *Wisconsin Magazine of History* 47 (1963): 12–25.

————. "Historical Perspective on Urban Development Schemes." In Leo Schnore and Henry Fagin, *Urban Research and Policy Planning, Urban Affairs Annual Reviews*, vol. 1, pp. 197–219. Beverly Hills, Calif.: Sage Publications, 1967.

Glaab, Charles N., and Brown, A. Theodore. *A History of Urban America.* New York: Macmillan Co., 1967.

Green, Constance McLaughlin. *American Cities in the Growth of the Nation.* New York: J. DeGraff, 1957.

————. *The Rise of Urban America.* New York: Harper & Row, 1965.

Handlin, Oscar. "The Modern City as a Field of Historical Study." In *The Historian and the City*, edited by Oscar Handlin and John Burchard, pp. 1–26. Cambridge: M.I.T. Press, 1963.

Hatt, Paul and Reiss, Jr., Albert. *Cities and Society: The Revised Reader in Urban Sociology.* Glencoe, Ill.: Free Press, 1957.

Hirsch, Mark D. "Reflections on Urban History and Urban Reform, 1865–1915." In *Essays in American Historiography: Papers Presented in Honor of Allan Nevins*, edited by D. H. Sheehan and H. C. Syrett. New York: Columbia University Press, 1960.

Holt, Glen E. "The Urban Negro American in the Twentieth Century: A Survey of Resources." In Doris B. Holleb, *Social and Economic Information for Urban Planning*, 2 vols., 2 : 295–312. Chicago: Center for Urban Studies, 1969.

Holt, W. Stull. "Some Consequences of the Urban Movement in American History." *Pacific Historical Review* 22 (1953): 337–51.

Hudson, Barbara J. "The City in America." *American Review* 2 (1962): 142–60.

Hoover, Dwight W. "The Diverging Paths of American Urban History." *American Quarterly* 20 (1968): 296–317.

Jackson, Kenneth T., and Schultz, Stanley K. *Urban America: The Historical Perspective.* New York: Alfred A. Knopf, 1970.

Lampard, Eric E. "American Historians and the Study of Urbanization." *American Historical Review* 67 (1961): 49–61.

Lipsett, Seymour Martin, and Hofstadter, Richard. *Sociology and History.* New York: Basic Books, 1968.

Lubove, Roy. "The Urbanization Process: An Approach to Historical Research." *Journal of the American Institute of Planners* 33 (1967): 33–39.

Marty, Martin E. "Bibliography on the History of the Churches of the American City." Typescript, available from author, 1967.

Mayer, Harold M., and Kohn, Clyde. *Readings in Urban Geography.* Chicago: University of Chicago Press, 1959.

McKelvey, Blake. "American Urban History Today." *American Historical Review* 57 (1952): 919–29.

———. *The Emergence of Metropolitan America, 1915–1966.* New Brunswick, N.J.: Rutgers University Press, 1968.

———. *The Urbanization of America.* New Brunswick, N.J.: Rutgers University Press, 1963.

———. "Urban Social and Economic Institutions in North America." *LaVille.* Vol. 7. Brussels, 1955.

Mumford, Louis. *The City in History: Its Origins, Its Transformations, and Its Prospects.* New York: Harcourt, Brace & World, 1961.

Pred, Allan R. *The Spatial Dynamics of U.S. Urban-Industrial Growth, 1800–1914: Interpretative and Theoretical Essays.* Cambridge: M.I.T. Press, 1966.

Schlesinger, Arthur. "The City in American History." *Mississippi Valley Historical Review* 27 (1940): 43–66.

———. "The City in American Civilization." In his *Paths to the Present*, pp. 210–33. New York: Macmillan Co., 1949.

———. *The Rise of the City, 1878–1898.* New York: Macmillan Co., 1933.

Smith, Wilson, ed. *Cities of Our Past and Present: A Descriptive Reader.* New York: John Wiley & Sons, 1964.

Speizman, Milton D., ed. *Urban America in the Twentieth Century.* New York: Thomas Y. Crowell Co., 1968.

Still, Bayrd. "History of the City in American Life." *American Review* 2 (1962): 142–60.

Still, Bayrd, and Klebanow, Diana. "The Teaching of American Urban History." *Journal of American History* 55 (March 1969): 843–47.

Strauss, Anselm L., ed. *The American City: A Sourcebook of Urban Imagery.* Chicago: Aldine Publishing Co., 1968.

———. *Images of the American City.* New York: Free Press of Glencoe, 1961.

Tager, Jack, and Goist, Park D. *The Urban Vision: Selected Interpretations of the Modern American City.* Homewood, Ill.: Dorsey Press, 1970.

Thernstrom, Stephan, and Sennett, Richard, eds. *Nineteenth-Century Cities: Essays in the New Urban History.* New Haven: Yale University Press, 1969.

Urban History Group. *Newsletter.* 1954 to present.

Wade, Richard C. "The City in History: Some American Perspectives." In *Urban Life and Form,* edited by Werner G. Hirsch. New York: Holt, Rinehart, & Winston, 1963.

———. "Urbanization." In *The Comparative Approach to American History,* edited by C. Vann Woodward, chap. 14. New York: Basic Books, 1968.

Wakstein, Allen M., ed. *The Urbanization of America: An Historical Anthology*. Boston: Houghton Mifflin Co., 1970.

Warner, Jr., Sam B. "If All the World Were Philadelphia: A Scaffolding for Urban History, 1774–1930." *American Historical Review* 74 (October 1958): 26–43.

Weimer, David R. *City and Country in America*. New York: Appleton-Century-Crofts, 1962.

Williamson, Jeffrey G., and Swanson, Joseph A. "The Growth of Cities in the American Northeast, 1820–1870." *Explorations in Entrepreneurial History*, Vol. 4, 2d ser. supplement (1966).

Wohl, R. Richard. "Urbanism, Urbanity and the Historian." *University of Kansas City Review*, October 1955, pp. 53–61.

Urban Transportation Records
in the National Archives

LEONARD RAPPORT

Because of the nature of our federal government the National Archives is not a prime source for records relating to urban transportation. A source for records of the train or bus that goes through the city, or the plane that lands at its airport, or the vessel that ties up at its docks, or the pipeline that serves it—yes. But for documentation about the subway, the urban bus, the trolley, the horsecar—a researcher's chances are better at home. It is not a hopeless cause, and I will get around to giving more information about records than a researcher may want to hear of. But records of urban transportation are not the strong suit. On the other hand, the National Archives offers a great deal of documentation about interstate transportation. There are whole stack areas where any box of records within reach is going to be pertinent to interstate transportation. But to find among the holdings those records relating to urban transportation is going to require some imagination—and some luck. In this search every man can be, almost has to be, his own historian. If he keeps panning he may get something, and, occasionally, he may find a real nugget. It is a challenging kind of search—if he likes and has time for challenges. He is always welcome at the National Archives; but, for his own good, if he is writing the history of the trolley company, he should exhaust the resources of Toonertown and of the state capital before coming to the National Archives.

What I will call to the attention of the researcher in urban transportation is only suggestive. I am identifying only the obvious, and, possibly the cream of what is in the National Archives. Despite this, any researcher may come at these collections and, using a different approach, find things I did not find. Why are there any urban transportation records at all in the National Archives? The Founding Fathers did not consider the subject and certainly did not write it into the Constitution. But they did consider and write into that document provisions that eventually resulted in the appearance of some documentation on urban transportation in the National Archives.

If the researcher runs through the Constitution he can see some of these provisions. For example, Congress is authorized to establish post offices and post roads. So the National Archives has the records of the Post Office Department. Is anyone interested in transporting things through six-inch pneumatic tubes? The records of the Pneumatic Tube Service go back almost eighty years and amount to almost fifty feet in storage space. The Constitution provides the authority that resulted in the establishment of the Patent Office. Undoubtedly much of the story of the development of the devices for moving people and things is documented in the records of this office. The Constitution also provides the authority to establish military forces. And so one finds among the Records of the Military Government of Cuba many letters received during the period 1899–1902 pertaining to the operation and construction of streetcars in Havana. The military have some other offerings. Quite early, from balloons and airplanes, military photographers were pointing cameras down at cities, particularly Washington. If one is interested in early traffic patterns or the parking situation, these photographs may be of interest. Some of the low-altitude shots give good close-ups of the streetcars. And other federal agencies made even better and more systematic surveys by air. The Constitution gives Congress exclusive jurisdiction over what is now the District of Columbia. The District is a city, an urban area, with all the transportation problems of other cities. Materials that reflect these problems in the Records of the Government of the District of Columbia are in the National Archives.

We have had a hasty run-through of some of the constitutional provisions that involve the federal government with urban transportation. There are other provisions that I have not as yet mentioned, among them those concerning the courts and commerce. Under the commerce clause of the Constitution the federal government does considerable regulating, and, in so doing, it sometimes touches on urban transportation. An obvious regulatory agency is the Interstate Commerce Commission. "Interstate" taken at face value almost rules out urban transportation. But in the ICC records there is material on urban transportation, which is stored among the thousands of feet of records and the tens of thousands of case files. I retrieved it by going down Pennsylvania Avenue to the ICC itself. In a couple of rooms next to the ICC library are batteries of cases of index cards. These are, as far as I know, used only by lawyers. This is too bad, because there are leads to intriguing materials in these indexes, which go back to 1887 and are arranged by locality, commodity, and subject. If one is interested in chautauquas or race horses or minstrel shows or stagecoaches—or anything else that traveled by land or connected with interstate carriers—he is likely to find one or more cards leading him to the original case files that are in the National Archives. And it is in these case files, not in the published findings, that one finds real substance. Does anyone want to know what it was like to get Jim Crowed before *Plessy v. Ferguson,* or exactly what a Jim Crow car on the predecessor of the Central of Georgia was like? Such information can be found in the earliest ICC case files. But the files also contain information on urban transportation.

Conflict between capital and labor generates case files and information. We have case files of the labor boards of both world wars, the National Labor Relations Board, and the Federal Mediation and Conciliation Service. For all of these there are both case files and other records pertaining to urban carriers. The records of the World War II Committee on Fair Employment Practice include case files pertaining to urban carriers in Philadelphia, Los Angeles, Washington, Oakland, and other cities.

Wartime emergency agencies are likely to get involved, for their own purposes, in urban transportation. In both world wars, particularly the first, the federal government actually took control of transportation systems to move defense workers to areas where they were needed. And the federal research agencies prepared studies of urban transportation in relation to defense needs. For example, in World War I, the United States Housing Corporation investigated transportation facilities and needs, negotiated with transportation companies for rearrangement of schedules, sometimes improved or even constructed facilities, and occasionally arranged financial help for needy companies.

The National Archives retains reports and studies done by investigatory agencies and by such special bodies as the United States Commission on Industrial Relations, 1912–15, which looked into the activities of urban transportation systems. It can even furnish such specialized information as the contents of vessel documents issued to passenger and freight ferries and other vessels that carry passengers and goods within the urban limits.

This is as far as I ought to go into these sources. I suggest that the researcher look at the staff paper prepared for this conference by Dr. George S. Ulibarri, entitled "Records in the National Archives Relating to Transportation in Chicago." Dr. Ulibarri discusses records in some record groups that I have omitted. What he found for Chicago a researcher may find, more or less, for other large cities.

The establishment of the Urban Mass Transportation Administration is going to change the picture somewhat. In 1961 the federal government began systematically to provide aid for mass transportation. The Urban Mass Transportation Act of 1964 greatly expanded the act of 1961 and authorized the first continuing federal program of mass transportation aid. In 1966 Congress expanded this program. In 1968 jurisdiction over the program was transferred from the Department of Housing and Urban Development to the new Department of Transportation, and the Urban Mass Transportation Administration was established. It is now coequal with the other administrations within the department that have a role in the regulation of surface, air, and water transport. With the coming of UMTA the government is now creating urban transportation records in large measure. For these records the National Archives will eventually be the prime depository.

PANEL ON THE IMPACT
OF FEDERAL ACTIVITIES

A Great Impact, A Gingerly Investigation: Historians and the Federal Effect on Urban Development

WILLIAM H. WILSON

In their study of cities, historians often profit from the work of students in other disciplines. In the area of the federal government's impact on urban development, historians' allies, the political scientists, have advanced useful generalizations which argue for the long duration, even the continuity, of some national stimulants to urban growth. The phrases "cooperative federalism," "shared functions," and "the marble cake of government" (as opposed to the theoretical "layer cake" denoting governmental activity in discrete spheres) all signify the mutual participation of federal, state, and local officials in important public enterprises.

An early example of this mixed government enterprise is the cooperative effort of the Richmond City Council and the Federal Board of Engineers of River and Harbor Improvements from 1853 through 1856. Similar joint local-federal financing of several kinds of internal improvements was commonplace in post-Civil War America. The airport and public housing programs of the 1930s are typical of more recent cooperative efforts.[1]

1. Daniel J. Elazar, "Urban Problems and the Federal Government: A Historical Inquiry," *Political Science Quarterly* 82 (December 1967): 505–25, is the most explicit study of historic federal-urban relationships. Elazar's study is reprinted in Alexander B. Callow, ed., *American Urban History: An Interpretive Reader with Commentaries* (New York: Oxford University Press, 1969), pp. 440–55. Subsequent citations are to the reprint. Elazar's notes are a good bibliography of published material on the subject. See also Elazar, *The American Partnership: Intergovernmental Co-operation in the Nineteenth-Century United States* (Chicago: University of Chicago Press, 1962), and "The Shaping of Intergovernmental Relations in the Twentieth Century," *Intergovernmental Relations in the United States, Annals of The American Academy of Political and Social Science* 359 (Philadelphia, May 1965): 10–22; Morton Grodzins, *The American System: A New View of Government in the United States*, ed. Daniel J. Elazar (Chicago: Rand McNally & Co., 1966), especially pp. v–xiv, 3–57; Roscoe C. Martin, *The Cities and the Federal System* (New York: Atherton Press, 1965), and "Washington and the Cities: An Introduction," in School of Government, Business, and International Affairs, George Washington University, *The Federal Government and the Cities* (Washington, D.C., 1961), pp. 1–15. Although it is more descriptive than theoretical, W. Brooke Graves, *American Intergovernmental Relations: Their*

The value that the political scientists' generalizations have for historians is the way they illuminate traditional federal-local relationships, whether or not those relationships involved "cooperative federalism" or "shared functions." The federal impact could be considerable even if the programs or functions were not designed to meet a specifically "urban" problem. For instance, during the nineteenth century the Post Office was a part of the community economic base, providing communications, cash, and rail and stage services bolstered by mail contracts. The United States Corps of Engineers aided cities and their regions with rivers and harbors—improvements actively sought by the municipalities. Canals, roads, and railroads, often federally assisted, bound cities into an urban transportation network. Many communities in the trans-Appalachian region benefited from townsite preemptions and federal land surveys. Other federal institutions aided local economies through contracts and payrolls including hospitals, customs offices, and military posts. Tariff policies were crucial for one-industry cities and towns. The relative importance of the older institutions, activities, and policies changed during the twentieth century, while new programs, such as federal highway construction, were added.[2]

Origins, Historical Development, and Current Status (New York: Charles Scribner's Sons, 1964), is a useful compendium. Graves concentrates on the post–World War II period. For federal-urban relations in earlier periods see pp. 655–59, 662–64, 861–63.

2. Few historians have acknowledged the work of Elazar and the others, and one who has done so in print has attacked "sharing." Harry N. Scheiber writes thoughtfully, but his criticisms of Elazar and others do not refute the argument that federal programs had a great impact on urban development. Scheiber bases his attack upon the relatively small (in terms of total state budgets) money and other grants to the states in the nineteenth century. He also discusses recent shifts of control over programs from state to federal hands, which are an argument against continuity. Scheiber's analysis ignores the types of federal "aid" to cities not shared with states, such as post office and military payrolls. Further, there is no necessary connection between the locus of power and the effect of a program upon urban growth. Some "traditional" federal activities with great effect were under federal control from the beginning. Finally, the federal share of a program did not have to consist of a large percentage of a state's budget over the years, or even in one year, in order to have a significant ·impact on the development of a city within the state. See Scheiber's "The Condition of American Federalism: An Historian's View," *The New Federalism,* ed. Frank Smallwood (Hanover, N.H.: Public Affairs Center, Dartmouth College, March 1967), pp. 19–55. The list of traditional activities follows Elazar, "Urban Problems and the Federal Government," pp. 444–47. Historical studies that acknowledge federal assistance to localities via internal improvements and the land laws include Paul W. Gates, *The Illinois Central Railroad and Its Colonization Work* (Cambridge: Harvard University Press, 1934); Carter Goodrich, ed., *Canals and American Economic Development* (New York: Columbia University Press, 1961); Forest G. Hill, *Roads, Rails, and Waterways: The Army Engineers and Early Transportation* (Norman: University of Oklahoma Press, 1957); W. Turrentine Jackson, *Wagon Roads West: A Study of Federal Road Surveys and Construction in the Trans-Mississippi West, 1846–1869* (New Haven: Yale University Press, 1965); Philip D. Jordan, *The National Road* (Indianapolis: Bobbs-Merrill Co., 1948); Richard C. Overton, *Burlington West: A Colonization History of the Burlington Railroad* (Cambridge: Harvard University

All these activities, from their beginnings through the New Deal, are gathered under the heading "traditional." The New Deal initiated path-breaking programs, it is true, but they are now as much a part of the governmental landscape as the older ones. Primary sources in the New Deal period are, generally speaking, as available as those for earlier eras.

It is much easier to say what those traditional activities were than it is to generalize about their effects on cities. Few of them have been closely examined. Some effects were indirect and difficult to measure. The increasing velocity of government at all levels has altered the relationships among federal activities and the cities over time. But at present two reasonably safe assumptions are that the federal impact on cities was significant from the early nineteenth century, and that it broadened dramatically in the years from 1933 to the Second World War. We may also assume that there was much more "sharing" in policy making and programs than the formal arrangements reveal. Informal "cooperative federalism" would be no less important or effective for its having operated through professional organizations, political parties, or the patronage.[3]

None of this should suggest that historians have ignored the impact of traditional federal activities on cities, but rather that their discussions of the impact often have been elliptical. This is true of urban biographies, and, with a few exceptions, of recent investigations of bossism and reform. It is also true of most computer-assisted research. The problem of reciprocal impact has received even less attention.

Urban biographies of the 1960s acknowledge the importance of federal land grants and expenditures. Federal spending of $3.8 million per year in the Kansas City region during the 1850s and federal aid to harbor and port facilities at Milwaukee and Houston during the nineteenth and early twen-

Press, 1941); John W. Reps, *The Making of Urban America: A History of City Planning in the United States* (Princeton: Princeton University Press, 1965), especially chap. 14; Roy M. Robbins, *Our Landed Heritage: The Public Domain, 1776–1936* (Princeton: Princeton University Press, 1942); Julius Rubin, *Canal or Railroad? Imitation and Innovation in the Response to the Erie Canal in Philadelphia, Baltimore, and Boston* (Philadelphia: American Philosophical Society, 1961); and Richard C. Wade, *The Urban Frontier: Pioneer Life in Early Pittsburgh, Cincinnati, Lexington, Louisville, and St. Louis* (Chicago: University of Chicago Press, 1964). Edward K. Muller, Department of Geography, University of Wisconsin, is studying the federal impact on urban development in Ohio before the Civil War. Muller to the author, April 11, 1970.

3. Urban historians are aware of the growing importance of the federal-urban relationship in the twentieth century, and especially after 1932. See, for example, Blake McKelvey, *The Emergence of Metropolitan America, 1915–1966* (New Brunswick, N.J.: Rutgers University Press, 1966), pp. 76–117; and Eric E. Lampard, "The Evolving System of Cities in the United States: Urbanizations and Economic Development," in *Issues in Urban Economics,* ed. Harvey S. Perloff and Lowden Wingo, Jr. (Baltimore: Johns Hopkins Press, 1968), p. 137. Elazar suggests the importance of informal sharing in "Urban Problems and the Federal Government," p. 445.

tieth centuries are examples of such assistance. Similarly, recent comparative studies mention federal benefits to cities and towns. Most of the Kansas cattle towns were founded under the national land laws. Two such towns, Dodge City and Ellsworth, benefited from nearby Army posts. Some citizens of antebellum southern Texas cities understood the importance of the federal impact. After the voters of San Antonio mustered a bare majority in favor of secession in 1861, the local newspaper warned of the loss of federal services and revenues. Unfortunately for our understanding of the federal impact, all of these instances are reported without much elaboration or generalization. An exception is Zane L. Miller's current research into urban blacks' experiences in southern cities during Reconstruction. Professor Miller has sifted the records of the Freedmen's Bureau and the Department of Justice and certainly will add to our understanding of the urban dimensions of these federal organizations. Generally speaking, both the single-city and the comparative studies continue to rely heavily upon local and regional sources. They emphasize local political, industrial and social developments, entrepreneurship, and urban rivalries.[4]

Local sources are valid, but overdependence upon them indicates a need for specialized studies such as Lucile M. Kane's *The Waterfall That Built a City* (1966). Less than an urban biography in scope, Miss Kane's work blends an account of federal participation in rebuilding and developing the Falls of St. Anthony at Minneapolis, beginning in 1870 and lasting through 1884, with subjects in the province of urban biography. The shrewd defense that Congressman Ignatius Donnelly of Minnesota made of federal appropriations (they were not simply to meet a private or local problem but to preserve a regional economy), the "sharing" of city and federal responsibilities, and twentieth-century federal improvements are recounted with the aid of records in the National Archives, including those of the Office of the Chief of Engineers. Other studies such as Miss Kane's could inform a new generation of urban biographers on the importance of federal work on rivers and harbors. Such monographs might also stimulate urban biographers to seek out evidence for other effects of federal impact on their cities.[5]

Authors of reexaminations of bossism and reform have used federal rec-

4. Bayrd Still, *Milwaukee: The History of a City* (Madison: State Historical Society of Wisconsin, 1965), pp. 44–46, 506–8; David G. McComb, *Houston: The Bayou City* (Austin: University of Texas Press, 1969), pp. 46–47, 93–97, 174; A. Theodore Brown, *Frontier Community: Kansas City to 1870* (Columbia, Mo.: University of Missouri Press, 1963), p. 14; Robert R. Dykstra, *The Cattle Towns* (New York: Alfred A. Knopf, 1968), pp. 12, 32, 42–45, 57, 63; and Kenneth W. Wheeler, *To Wear a City's Crown: The Beginnings of Urban Growth in Texas, 1836–1865* (Cambridge: Harvard University Press, 1968), p. 154. Zane L. Miller, University of Cincinnati, to the author, May 11, 1970.

5. Lucile Kane, *The Waterfall That Built a City* (St. Paul: Minnesota Historical Society, 1966), pp. 64–65, 75–80, 130–33, 168–71. For use of National Archives material see p. 182. Marilyn McAdams Sibley's capable book, *The Port of Houston: A*

ords to better advantage than authors of most urban biographies. These recent studies by younger scholars have shown both bosses and reformers responding to the rapid growth and inadequate political structures of cities, seeking to rationalize urban government and appeal to all, or nearly all, of the urban class interests. Several of these students have used federal sources to illuminate local problems, but two authors in particular promise to clarify significant relationships between urban bosses and the federal government.[6]

Joel A. Tarr's examinations of boss politics and political banking in Chicago demonstrate a close connection between political banks and the Office of the Comptroller of the Currency. Political banks were those owned by politicians such as William Lorimer or by politically oriented financiers. They depended upon their owners' followings and public funds for deposits. They loaned funds to favored individuals or to other businesses controlled by their owners. Prudent management was hardly a hallmark of such banks. Personal notes were often poorly secured, and company bonds of dubious value were listed among bank assets. This does not mean that the comptroller of the currency connived at these practices, for they sometimes conflicted with the comptroller's policies. Examiners of banks under the National Banking System condemned political banks in their reports. Yet it is doubtful whether the Windy City boss Lorimer ever would have received a national bank charter had he not been a United States senator at the time he applied for one. Because he was a senator, the comptroller waived the usual investigation.[7]

Professor Tarr's examination of the comptroller's records suggests that a good deal of information regarding politicians' use of federal departments and agencies for local purposes may be as yet undiscovered in the National Archives. The records of the Post Office Department and the records of the office of the Chief of Engineers, among others, may contain references to "federal aid" for urban politicians.

History (Austin: University of Texas Press, 1968), did not cite National Archives records, nor did it inspire as much originality in the research and writing of McComb, *Houston,* as it should have.

6. Recent bossism-and-reform studies include Alexander B. Callow, Jr., *The Tweed Ring* (New York: Oxford University Press, 1966; James B. Crooks, *Politics and Progress: The Rise of Urban Progressivism in Baltimore, 1895 to 1911* (Baton Rouge: Louisiana State University Press, 1960); Melvin G. Holli, *Reform in Detroit: Hazen S. Pingree and Urban Politics* (New York: Oxford University Press, 1969); Zane L. Miller, *Boss Cox's Cincinnati: Urban Politics in the Progressive Era* (New York: Oxford University Press, 1968); and Jack Tager, *The Intellectual as Urban Reformer: Brand Whitlock and the Progressive Movement* (Cleveland: Press of Case Western Reserve University, 1968).

7. Joel A. Tarr, "J. R. Walsh of Chicago: A Case Study in Banking and Politics, 1881–1905," *Business History Review* 40 (Winter 1966): 451–66; A Study in Boss Politics: William Lorimer of Chicago (Urbana: University of Illinois Press, 1971), pp. 231–32; 309–13.

Lyle Dorsett's analysis of Kansas City, Missouri, boss politics offers abundant proof that federal aid to city machines grew with the development of federal functions. In *The Pendergast Machine* Professor Dorsett concluded that the New Deal greatly aided the Kansas City organization by awarding to Thomas Pendergast the local control over its unprecedented relief and reconstruction programs. Harry Hopkins funneled CWA funds into the city through the Pendergast organization. Within a few days after the WPA was established, Hopkins placed Kansas City's director of public works at the head of federal public works in Missouri. For a few years thereafter WPA workers were cleared through boss Pendergast's machine before being hired and were expected to vote for local and statewide Pendergast candidates. Thus the New Deal scarcely undermined the boss by gathering welfare and relief into its own hands at his expense.

Bruce M. Stave reached similar conclusions in his study, *The New Deal and the Last Hurrah: Pittsburgh Machine Politics*. Before the New Deal the Democratic party in Pennsylvania's second city was a pathetic, timeserving adjunct of the Republican machine. So few Democrats were registered in some districts that Republicans obliged by sitting as election judges for the Democratic party. The party blossomed rapidly under the "Hoover depression" and the warmth of Roosevelt's personality. Although an eccentric Democratic mayor reduced the flow of federal funds to Pittsburgh for a time, after the autumn of 1936 Democratic regulars were feeding at the federal welfare trough. Places on the WPA for party workers, patronage, and other aids helped to build Democratic strength during the New Deal years.

The Dorsett and Stave books challenge the argument—eloquently stated in Edwin O'Connor's novel *The Last Hurrah*—that New Deal welfare programs caused the urban masses to look to Washington and not to local politicians for handouts. Roosevelt eventually broke with Pendergast, but only because revelations of fraud and corruption weakened the paunchy boss within his own bailiwick. The Pittsburgh Democratic machine originally fashioned by David L. Lawrence eventually lost a primary fight to insurgent reformers, but that was in 1969 and the loss had little to do with the New Deal.

In the WPA files in the National Archives there are letters detailing the bosses' use of federal jobs for political ends. At the Roosevelt Library the files of the Democratic National Committee and the personal papers of the president, Louis Howe, Harry Hopkins, and others, reveal the close relationships between New Deal leaders and the machines.[8]

Federal sources, especially census information, are the fulcrum of schol-

8. Lyle Dorsett, *The Pendergast Machine* (New York: Oxford University Press, 1968), pp. 102–17, 131–32. Bruce M. Stave, *The New Deal and the Last Hurrah: Pittsburgh Machine Politics* (Pittsburgh: University of Pittsburgh Press, 1970), pp. 162–82, 245. Dorsett, University of Missouri at St. Louis, to the author, March 2,

ars involved in what Samuel P. Hays has termed "historical social research." Despite this, many of these computer-assisted quantitative studies of ethnic voting, occupational mobility, and urban residential patterns do not consider the possibilities of a federal impact upon their topics. Some types of federal activity are difficult to quantify, and, as one student notes, "the tie-ins for federal activities are infinite." Despite the difficulties there are certain federal influences amenable to analysis. Prof. Michael H. Ebner found a correlation between population increases in Passaic, New Jersey, and the growth of the city's postal service while completing his dissertation on Passaic from the mid-nineteenth century to 1912. The post office hired immigrant clerks to decipher the foreign mail to Passaic mill workers, and provided job mobility for at least one leader of the Slavic community. As a reward for his services to the Republican party, the leader was appointed a clerk in the post office branch serving his fellow Slavs. The Ebner findings suggest that the authors of the large number of mobility studies now under way might well consider the influence of federal employment, including employment by federal contractors, upon mobility.[9]

The research of Lawrence J. Golicz in the development of Bangor, Maine, indicates some other possibilities for historical social research blended with traditional techniques. Professor Golicz predicts that the records of the Post Office Department and of the Bureau of Customs in the National Archives will yield valuable material on the development of business activity. Bangor was an important port in the lumber and dry goods trade and had a large post office in the nineteenth century. Relocation of the post office in 1912 involved municipally owned land. Because Bangor is a tidal upriver port there may be useful material on fluvial problems in the records of the Office of the Chief of Engineers.[10]

Thus far we have assumed that federal activity influenced urban development, but research in post office operations demonstrates how the influences were reciprocal, and how urban developments forced innovation and experiment in traditional federal functions. Carl H. Scheele describes these influences in his *A Short History of the Mail Service* (1970), a study resting in part upon sources in the National Archives. Read in one way, much of Mr. Scheele's book is an account of one federal department's desperate ef-

1970, and March, n.d., 1970. Constance McLaughlin Green, *The Rise of Urban America* (New York: Harper & Row, 1965), accepts the *Last Hurrah* thesis, pp. 170–71.

9. Samuel P. Hays, "The Use of Archives for Historical Statistical Inquiry," *Prologue: The Journal of the National Archives* 1 (Fall 1969): 7–15. Lawrence J. Golicz, University of Maine, to the author, April 6, 1970. Two path-breaking studies virtually ignore the federal influence: Stephan Thernstrom, *Poverty and Progress: Social Mobility in a Nineteenth Century City* (Cambridge: Harvard University Press, 1964), and Sam Bass Warner, Jr., *The Private City: Philadelphia in Three Periods of Its Growth* (Philadelphia: University of Pennsylvania Press, 1968). Ebner to the author, April 10, 1970, Herbert H. Lehman College, Bronx, N. Y.

10. Golicz to author, April 6, 1970.

forts to keep pace with urban sprawl, crowding, increasingly clogged streets, mounting volumes of interurban and intraurban mail to be collected, sorted, and delivered, and importunities from urban businessmen for improved service.

As early as 1829 the Boston Post Office employed one or more letter carriers to distribute mail to residents who otherwise would have had to call at the post office. During the Civil War, Congress extended "free letter carrier service" to forty-nine cities and towns, twenty-eight years before Postmaster General John Wanamaker's experiments in rural free delivery, and thirty-three years before RFD became an American institution. When "special delivery" was introduced in 1885 it was essentially an urban service.

The 1890s saw remarkable innovations in the Post Office Department's struggle with the flood of mail. White-painted streetcar railway post offices appeared on the trolley tracks of eleven large cities during the last decade of the nineteenth century. The service was effective, but it expanded to only a few additional cities before the ubiquitous motor truck began displacing it. Experiments with horseless mail wagons began in 1899, when they cut the collection time of horse-drawn wagons in half. By 1910 trucks were an established part of the urban post office scene.

Postal pneumatic tubes to speed intracity mail below choked streets were a novel solution to the problems of mail flow. Begun in Philadelphia in 1893, the system spread to other urban areas until, in 1915, the Post Office Department rented 56.5 miles of tubes, of which almost twenty-nine miles were in New York City. The tubes were rented at fancy figures from their builders, they carried only envelopes and very small packages, they gave the mails a rough ride, and they were doomed by the department's fondness for automobiles. Yet, New York City's lines alone could move 6 million letters daily at an average speed of thirty-five miles per hour. These and many other innovations are evidence for Mr. Scheele's assertion that "The rising tide of mail seemed to take on the personality of a demon who furiously and relentlessly beat at the post office door."

Of course, the post office affected the cities, too. For example, in the 1920s the department refused to establish or extend city delivery routes unless cities supplied sidewalks, street signs, and other "civic improvements." One wonders whether other federal agencies might have forced some of the social costs of their services upon urban governments. Yet the primary image of the Post Office Department planners is that of men on an accelerating treadmill of urban growth, running faster and faster to stay in place. Urban expansion may have had similar effects on other traditional federal functions, but the research required to discover them remains to be done.[11]

11. Carl H. Scheele, *A Short History of the Mail Service* (Washington, D.C.: Smithsonian Institute Press, 1970), pp. 66, 91–92, 106, 128–30, 131–35, 136–38, 140.

The recent and present research in the history of single cities or groups of cities, in bossism and reform, in historical social problems, and in the operations of government departments will surely inspire other studies and will end in the invalidation of the title of this paper. Yet one of the most potentially fruitful areas remains relatively untapped. Historians are agreed that the New Deal greatly expanded the relationships between urban and federal governments. Research materials are available in abundant quality and quantity. We know in a general way that many New Deal programs were urban oriented. For example, the WPA's Federal Theatre Project concentrated its brilliantly innovative productions in the largest cities. Its emphasis on the development of "regional theatre" usually meant theatre in important regional cities. Small-town audiences saw marionette shows and decrepit soft-shoe routines, but rarely any major drama. There was a lot of "back to the land" rhetoric in the New Deal community planning program but "the three largest, most ambitious, and most significant communities of the New Deal" were the Greenbelt towns. These planned suburbs absorbed one-third of the program's funds and one-fourth of its settlers. The housing program was potentially much more important than resettlement. One student observes that through housing legislation "the federal government could now for the first time, if it wished, measurably influence the shape of urban development."

Despite the New Deal's concern about cities, few studies of the Roosevelt administration focus even briefly on federal-urban relationships. Professor Dorsett's analysis of bossism and the New Deal shows how some clichés about the New Deal's political impact need to be revised. Roscoe C. Martin's review of federal aid to civil aviation in his *The Cities and the Federal System*, though less satisfactory for an historian, reveals a medley of city-based organizations besieging the federal government for funds, urging it to establish direct connections between federal officials and their local counterparts. The organizations wished to bypass the states.[12]

Most "nationwide" improvements were really improvements in intercity mail service. The quotation is from Scheele's paper, "The Post Office Department and Urban Congestion, 1893–1953" (read at the annual meeting of the American Historical Association, Toronto, December 1967). See also Wayne E. Fuller, *RFD: The Changing Face of Rural America* (Bloomington, Ind.: Indiana University Press, 1964), pp. 116–18, 155, 233–47, 249–58, 259–86. The reciprocal impact had social, intellectual, and political, as well as administrative overtones. J. Joseph Huthmacher's studies indicate the possibilities for examinations of the reciprocal impact. See "Urban Liberalism and the Age of Reform," *Mississippi Valley Historical Review* 49 (September 1962): 231–41, and *Senator Robert F. Wagner and the Rise of Urban Liberalism* (New York: Atheneum, 1968).

12. Jane DeHart Mathews, *The Federal Theatre, 1935–1939* (Princeton: Princeton University Press, 1967), pp. 84–86, 179–80; Paul K. Conkin, *Tomorrow a New World: The New Deal Community Planning Program* (Ithaca, N.Y.: Cornell University Press, 1959), p. 305. Roscoe C. Martin, *The Cities and the Federal System* (New York:

As the Martin book suggests, the New Deal years coincided with a general realization that urban problems were national problems requiring federal action. The growth of national organizations designed, among other reasons, to raise the voice of the nation's cities at the federal capital was another phenomenon of the 1930s. These developments are among many changes in the scope and scale of the New Deal generation's understanding of, and attack upon, urban difficulties.

Studies of the New Deal and the cities should divert us from viewing the New Deal primarily in terms of federal-state relationships. Books on intergovernmental relations written from the federal-state viewpoint do explain a great deal. They also obscure much when they stretch the poor little word "local" to fit every government below the state level, whether at a crossroads or a metropolis. For example, from their fresh perspective the federal-city studies might examine the current assumption that New Deal spending was a uniformly good thing for the cities and their residents. Sam B. Warner, Jr., has suggested that it was not. According to Professor Warner, the New Deal dealt a heavy blow to urban bureaucracies already crippled by the loss of taxable wealth to the suburbs and by the public's demands for minimum services cheaply rendered. The New Deal recruited its own bureaucracy from local ranks, while it dumped money on the depleted urban governments. As a result, Professor Warner writes, the understaffed city administrations wasted much of the federal largess.

Happily, Mark L. Gelfand's dissertation tentatively titled "A Nation of Cities" will address itself to some current points of dispute while it examines still other New Deal contributions. These contributions include "Our Cities," the report of the Urbanism Committee of the National Resources Committee, "the first major national study of cities in the United States." The Gelfand study ranges through a variety of manuscripts, including material in the National Archives.[13]

The National Archives and Records Service has placed historians of federal-urban relationships in deep debt to it for preserving the records of tradi-

Atherton Press, 1965), pp. 83–108. The quotation is from Mark L. Gelfand, Columbia University, to the author, May 15, 1970.

13. James T. Patterson, in *The New Deal and the States: Federalism in Transition* (Princeton: Princeton University Press, 1969), suggests important relationships between urbanism and the New Deal but the major theme overshadows his suggestions. See pp. 162–64, 170–72, 184–85, 190–91, 207. For generally favorable views of New Deal activity see Kane, *Waterfall That Built a City*, p. 174, and Still, *Milwaukee*, pp. 482–84, 498–501, 506–8, 511–13, 547–48. See Warner's "Urban Constraints and Federal Policy" in his *Planning for a Nation of Cities* (Cambridge: M.I.T. Press, 1966), especially pp. 50–52. Gelfand's dissertation is under the direction of William E. Leuchtenberg of Columbia University. Its full title: "A Nation of Cities: The Federal Government's Response to the Challenges of Urban America, 1933–1965." Warner deplores the federal government's role in urban freeway construction in his *The Urban Wilderness: A History of the American City* (New York: Harper & Row, 1972), pp. 37–52.

tional federal activities involving the cities. Historians scarcely could ask for more attention to collection and preservation. There is much to be done at the local level, but the problems there are not the responsibility of the National Archives. Yet some serious difficulties surrounding the availability of records remain. Professor Tarr found the restrictions on confidential federal bank examiners' reports extended while he was conducting his research into political banking in Chicago. The extension later was reversed, but the incident points up the need for historians to make known their views respecting the problems of confidentiality imbedded in the present laws. For another example, the law may prevent the release of the 1900 and subsequent manuscript census records. If the manuscript records remain closed, historical studies of twentieth-century cities will be crippled.

At the same time historians perhaps could be educated about the problems of privacy involved in releasing census material. The historian who demands to use the 1900 census data and who scoffs at concern for the privacy of turn-of-the-century citizens may be the same fellow who, in April 1970, questioned the government's right to inquire whether or not he enjoyed the comforts of a flush toilet. We might well ask ourselves how we would answer the census takers, knowing that the graduate students of our graduate students' graduate students (our great-great grad. students?) will be poring over our returns. At any rate, representatives from our profession and from the National Archives ought to face this and similar problems together, and have them constantly under review. The federal government has had, and will have, a great impact on our cities, and urban historians must have the sources with which to gauge that impact.[14]

14. Joel A. Tarr, "A Historian and the Federal Government," *Pacific Historical Review* 38 (August 1969): 329–35. James B. Rhoads to Tarr, December 23, 1969, copy, Records Appraisal Division, National Archives Building. Edwin D. Goldfield, "Preservation of Confidential Records," *Historical Methods Newsletter* 2 (December 1968), and comment, pp. 2–6.

Selected Policy Measures Relating to Urban Development

GERALD L. DUSKIN

National concern with urban-oriented problems and programs has never been so great as it has been in the past several years. Almost every part of the federal administration is carrying out, or at least planning, one or more programs aimed at aiding cities and other urban areas. Much of this concern has stemmed from the belief that the patterns of population shifts may be harming rural areas and simultaneously aggravating urban problems. Regardless of what is done, massive population growth is going to take place and practically all of it will mean an increase in the number of urban areas.

POPULATION GROWTH AND CONCENTRATION

At the time of the first census in 1970, 95 percent of the people lived on farms or in places of less than 2,500 inhabitants. Only 5 percent lived in urban places of 2,500 inhabitants or more. The rapid growth of urban areas is a relatively recent phenomenon. It was only in the 1920s that the percentage of people residing in urban areas began to exceed 50 percent.[1] Total United States population in May 1969 is estimated to be slightly over 205 million. More than 70 percent of the population now lives in urban places, and nearly 65 percent in metropolitan areas.[2] The metropolis or Standard

1. Urban areas, according to the 1960 census definition, consist of (a) incorporated places of 2,500 inhabitants or more; (b) the densely settled urban fringe, incorporated or not, or urban areas; (c) towns in New England and townships in New Jersey and Pennsylvania that have either 25,000 inhabitants or more or a population of 2,500 to 25,000 and a density of 1,500 persons per square mile; counties elsewhere, with no incorporated municipalities, that have a density of 1,500 persons or more per square mile; (d) unincorporated places of 2,500 inhabitants or more. U.S., Department of Commerce, Bureau of the Census, *Statistical Abstract of the United States: 1969*, 90th ed. (Washington, D.C., 1969).

2. In 1960, according to the census, 69.9 percent lived in urban places, and 63 percent lived in metropolitan areas. Bureau of the Census, *Statistical Abstract of the United States: 1969*.

Metropolitan Statistical Area[3] has come to characterize the pattern of settlement in this nation.

Urbanization is neither evenly distributed among metropolitan areas nor among regions. According to Patricia L. Hodge and Philip M. Hauser in a report prepared for the National Commission on Urban Problems,[4] out of a total of more than two hundred SMSAs in 1960, almost 30 percent of the metropolitan area population lived in the five SMSAs of 3 million or more; approximately 25 percent lived in the nineteen SMSAs of 1 million to 3 million; thus, more than half the 1960 metropolitan population lived in twenty-four SMSAs. In contrast there were twenty-two SMSAs of less than 100,000 in population in 1960 within which less than 2 percent *of all metropolitan* residents resided.

The actual geographic distribution of the population is the result of millions of individual location decisions. Although personal economic incentive, better jobs and income are clearly important factors in making people decide whether or not to move and where, other factors clearly enter in, such as climate, age, family and community ties, unemployment insurance, and individual attitudinal traits. In the case of some groups such as Negroes, attitudes towards social and political conditions are key factors.

An important factor in the composition of recent population trends and a major dimension of recent urbanization has been the migration of the Negroes from the rural South to large cities. Statistically, the Negro population in this country has become more urbanized and more metropolitan than the white population. In 1969, 70 percent of all Negroes lived in metropolitan areas, compared to 64 percent for the white population.[5] Almost all Negro population growth is occurring within metropolitan areas, primarily within central cities. From 1950 to 1966, the Negro population rose 6.5 million. Over 98 percent of that rise took place in metropolitan areas—86 percent within central cities, 12 percent in the urban fringe. During the same period, 78 percent of the white population increase of 35.6 million took

3. A Standard Metropolitan Statistical Area is "a county or group of contiguous counties (except in New England) which contains at least one central city of 50,000 inhabitants or more or 'twin cities' with a combined population of at least 50,000. In addition, other contiguous counties are included in an SMSA if, according to certain criteria, they are essentially metropolitan in character and are socially and economically integrated with the central city. In New England, towns and cities rather than counties are used in defining SMSAs." Bureau of the Census, *Statistical Abstract of the United States: 1969*, p. 2.

4. Patricia L. Hodge and Philip M. Hauser, "The Challenge of America's Metropolitan Population: 1960 to 1985," Research Report no. 3 prepared for the National Commission on Urban Problems (Washington, D.C.: Government Printing Office, 1968), p. 83.

5. U.S., Department of Commerce, Bureau of the Census, *Population of the United States by Metropolitan–Non-metropolitan Residence, 1969 and 1960,* Current Population Reports, Series P–20, no. 197 (Washington, D.C., March 6, 1970).

place in the suburbs, while central cities received only 2.5 percent of this total white increase. Since 1960, white central city population has actually declined.[6]

The net Negro migration out of the South between 1940 and 1950 was 1.6 million; from 1950 to 1960, 1.5 million; and from 1960 to 1966, 613,000.[7] Since 1966 the rush has slowed significantly, to slightly more than one-half the 1950–60 annual rate.[8]

A recent report by the Advisory Commission on Intergovernmental Relations underscores two significant urbanization trends: the growing importance of the natural increase component to overall population growth in metropolitan areas and the concentration of population growth that has been taking place in just a very few metropolitan areas.[9] In the period between 1960 and 1965, natural increases accounted for 78 percent of metropolitan population growth, while net migration accounted for 22 percent of aggregate net growth. These proportions differ significantly with the 65 percent– 35 percent breakdown for the preceding decade from 1950 to 1960. The significance of this change can be explained in terms of the larger total part of the population that metropolitan areas are assuming. During the 1960–65 period, eleven metropolitan areas[10] registered a total population increase of 5.1 million or 46 percent of total growth for all metropolitan areas. These eleven areas had population increases ranging from 205,000 for Dallas to more than 1.1 million for Los Angeles-Orange County. Sixty-two percent of the total increase resulted from natural increase and 38 percent from inmigration. It should be noted that the South and West accounted for seven of the eleven areas. The net effect of these trends is that while shifts of population to the more rapidly expanding regional economies of the South and West has enhanced the growth and regional convergence of income levels in the nation as a whole, the counterflow of Negro migration, supplemented by natural increase, the main source of Negro central city population rise, has created expanding ghettos in the larger, older cities of the Northeast and North-Central regions.

6. *Report of the National Advisory Commission on Civil Disorders*, (Washington, D.C., March 1968), p. 118.

7. Ibid., p. 117.

8. U.S., Bureau of the Census, U.S. Bureau of Labor Statistics, *Recent Trends in Social and Economic Conditions of Negroes in the United States,* Current Population Reports, Series P-23, no. 26. Bureau of Labor Statistics Report no. 347, (Washington, D.C., July 1968).

9. Advisory Commission on Intergovernmental Relations, *Urban and Rural America: Policies for Future Growth,* A-32 (Washington, D.C., April 1968), p. 16.

10. Los Angeles-Orange County; New York-northeastern New Jersey; Detroit; Chicago; San Francisco-Oakland-San Jose; Washington, D.C.; Philadelphia; Houston; Miami-Fort Lauderdale; San Bernardino-Riverside; Dallas.

THE CHANGING ECONOMIC FORM AND STRUCTURE
OF METROPOLITAN AREAS

In recent decades of the postwar period our metropolitan areas have been experiencing profound changes in their economic structure and form. The manifestation of these changes is the decline of the central city and the accelerated growth of the suburban ring immediately surrounding the central city. While population and employment in the suburban ring have grown phenomenally in recent years, population and employment in the central cities have failed to grow significantly and in many metropolitan areas have declined absolutely. This decentralization can be illustrated by looking at the changes in the forty largest metropolitan areas. Between 1950 and 1960 more than half the central cities of these areas experienced population declines. Retailing employment located in the central cities fell from almost 75 percent in 1948 to just over half the total retailing employment by the mid-1960s. Whereas only one-tenth of the total wholesaling employment was located in the suburban ring in 1947, by the mid-1960s one-third of the total was located in the ring. Of total selected services employment, 36 percent was in the surburban ring in mid-1960s compared with only 18 percent in 1948.[11]

Concomitant with the growth of the suburban ring at the expense of the central city has been the virtual entrapment of the poor, particularly the Negro, whose chances of participating in employment growth—frequently restricted by discrimination—are further diminished by lack of information and difficulties in commuting to jobs in the suburban ring.

The underlying cause of these changes in the spatial distribution of population and employment is the result of (1) a complex of changes that have been taking place in patterns of consumption and living, in transportation and communications technology, and in production technology and distribution; and (2) federal programs that have had a significant effect on the location of population and economic activity in the suburban ring, frequently resulting in the decline of the central city.

Changes in patterns of consumption and living have come about as the result of rising incomes, increasing availability of automobiles, and mass production. Rising incomes have enabled city dwellers to purchase single-family dwellings, while the automobile has made it feasible for these dwellings to be located in low-density residential areas. The rise of suburban living, accompanied by greater purchasing power and mobility through use of automobiles, has been followed by dispersal of retailing and service employ-

11. John F. Kain, *The Distribution and Movement of Jobs and Industry* (Cambridge: M.I.T., Harvard Joint Center for Urban Studies, 1966).

ment. Many retailing and service activities, especially those which deal in goods and services of small unit cost and which require little mechanization, have traditionally followed population movements, but in addition to changes in population distribution, the increase in the numbers of suburbanites has meant enhanced purchasing power at the outskirts of the city, and the automobile has provided the mobility and flexibility that has made shopping centers feasible.

Changes in transportation technology have had the effect of making land in different sections of the metropolitan area more homogeneous and thereby have lessened the need of industrial firms for central locations near rail or port facilities. Transportation facilities are now less likely to be located in central cities, but are in many cases being transferred to points of intersection of rail lines and circumferential highways.

Changes in production technology are yet another factor in decentralization of employment. Continuous processes and automatic handling equipment are not feasible in multistoried buildings, but require sprawling, one-storied buildings. The lower real estate values and the availability of large, unencumbered tracts on the fringes of the city are thus preferable to central city locations that are restricted by their block layouts.

Suburban locations are as likely as central city locations to attract their required labor forces, if not more likely.

Changes in communications technology have reduced the need for locating all functional activities in one location and have made it more feasible to locate different functions about the metropolitan areas at points of maximum advantage rather than in the central city.

The growth in manpower skills and educational attainment of the labor force have led employers to upgrade job requirements with real wages, but this has tended to constrain the availability of jobs for the less-qualified urban ghetto labor force. The high unemployment rates cannot be regarded, however, as simply the result of the lack of sufficient jobs in the ghetto, but rather as the result of the inability of ghetto residents to participate fully in the rapid growth of the suburban ring. Employment is being pulled by inexorable centrifugal forces to the suburban ring, while the level and distribution of ghetto resident employment is being restricted by housing and employment discrimination.

The result of these changes has been to produce what Professor Kain has referred to as a "doughnut" structure, in which employment growth is concentrated in the suburban ring while the central city decays. But while the decentralization of employment has been accompanied by decentralization of white population, the poor have been entrapped in the central city ghettos and thus isolated to an extent from employment growth. As the problem deepens, still more middle- and upper-income families move to the suburbs.

The problem is also one of obsolescence of physical plant and the consequent deterioration of the city into a haven of the aged, public assistance recipients and other "high-cost" citizens. (The 1970 census will provide new opportunities to investigate these problems. For example, it will provide considerably more systematic information on place of work and place of residence than it did in the past. This new data should permit us to gain a better understanding of the metropolitan labor market and the way limitations in the housing market affect the employment opportunities of minorities.)

Federal programs have had a significant effect on the location of population and economic activity and the character of urban development. The FHA mortgage insurance program makes it easier for people to buy new homes, thereby inducing them to move to the suburbs and outlying areas. This move frequently results in increased sprawl. Federal procurement, particularly for defense and space exploration, will finance the location or relocation of entire industrial complexes from high-density areas to the outlying portions of metropolitan or subregional areas.

Under the federal highway program, express highways are constructed that are supposed to make it simpler for commuters to move back and forth from the suburb to the central city; and to commute between their homes and the suburban place of work and the suburban shopping centers. The coming of the expressways, especially the limited-access roads of the 1950s, permitted the development of urban sprawl. Also, the highway-stimulated outward movements have contributed to making commuting distances longer and time loss greater and costs higher. In fact, the cost of urban freeway construction varies directly with population density of the areas affected and inversely with distance.

Thus we see that these and other programs have worked at cross purposes, exacerbating the problem of the cities. In recent years, however, major national programs have been redirected to favor cities. The cities' share of federally aided housing, federally aided highways, urban renewal and Model Cities programs, federal aid to mass transit and other federal expenditures and grants and loan programs is rising. New approaches to the economic development of the cities, including industrial promotion incentives and industrial parks, represent an important new effort to add an essential margin of jobs to cities.

CURRENT FEDERAL PROGRAMS FOR URBAN DEVELOPMENT

I have not attempted to add up all the various forms of federal financial commitment for urban social and community development aids. One of the more recent estimates puts the total at $33 billion for 1968, nearly double the level of 1961. I would speculate it may be somewhat larger today.

The scope of federal programs that bear on urban development is indicated by the following funding levels for fiscal year 1969:

A. Research, development, and planning to provide new knowledge and methods to assist and guide program operations—$214 million.
    (See the Appendix to this paper, item 1.)

B. Programs to provide loans, grants, and technical assistance for the renewal, rehabilitation, and public works facilities for improvement of neighborhoods, communities, local subdivisions, states, and Indian reservations—$541 million.
    (See Appendix, item 2.)

C. Programs to provide financial assistance through grants and loans to businesses to assist private initiative and capital in bringing about industrial and commercial growth—$648 million.
    (See Appendix, item 3.)

D. Programs for manpower development and training for the disadvantaged worker, including funding for research and demonstration grants for employment, unemployment, underemployment, training, and mobility projects—$542 million.
    (See Appendix, item 4. Refer to item 5 for a description of the technical assistance and services program. The amounts given under this heading are incomplete, and for that reason item 5 is excluded from this listing.)

E. Programs to provide capital grants and loans for mass transportation for improving service, minimizing costs, and upgrading facilities and equipment—$237 million.
    (See Appendix, item 6.)

Federal Grants-in-Aid

Federal grants-in-aid to state and local governments in fiscal 1969 exceeded $20 billion, exactly double what they were five years earlier. In January 1966, the latest date for which an actual count has been made, there were 162 major grant programs. In many cases, individual programs have within them several different types of grant authorizations—for training, for operations, for research, and so forth. In early 1966, the number of these grant authorizations was 400.[12] Presumably, these grant programs were not designed simply to provide generalized financial assistance to state and local governments. Each is the result of a relatively complex piece of legislation,

12. U.S., Bureau of the Budget, *Special Analyses: Budget of the United States, Fiscal Year 1969* (1968), p. 164.

aimed at a particular set of objectives. In some cases, federal programs have been directed toward purposes for which state and local governments have historically spent little funds. In these situations federal funds for a particular purpose have undoubtedly been effective in increasing total resources devoted to that purpose. The program of the Office of Economic Opportunity to provide legal services for the poor is such an example.

As mentioned, there are more than 160 federal programs of assistance to states and localities, administered through nearly 400 separate authorizations. Confronted by this multiplicity of choices, a community must carefully decide which programs will best suit its needs. One way for it to decide is for it to analyze a selected target area, determine what the array of problems is, and formulate a plan of action for attacking the problems simultaneously, using an appropriate combination of local, state, federal and private resources.

A community's analysis might reveal that the problems of an inner-city, low-income area are interrelated: that in the substandard housing live families whose economic level will not permit them to live elsewhere; that these families depend on public assistance or on a low-wage breadwinner; that children of these families attend schools that are run-down, overcrowded, understaffed, and ill-equipped; or that persons may have to go some distance outside the area to the nearest health facilities. It may further be revealed that there are no recreational facilities, and that school dropouts are either ignorant of or cynical about training opportunities.

The interrelationships of the various problems indicate that a viable solution must present a several-pronged but coordinated program of attack that includes upgrading housing, improving related public facilities, and improving social services. But what usually takes place is a fragmented approach to the problem. Federal programs often seem self-defeating and contradictory; agencies are unable or unwilling to work together; programs are conceived and administered to achieve different and sometimes conflicting purposes. The National Advisory Commission on Civil Disorders found that between 1961 and 1965 almost twenty executive orders were issued for the coordination of federal programs involving intergovernmental administration.[13] Some two dozen interagency committees were established to coordinate two or more federal aid programs. Departments have been given responsibility to lead others in areas within their particular competence. Yet, according to the advisory commission, despite these efforts, the federal government has not been able to join talent, funds, and programs for a concentrated impact. If essential programs are to be preserved, systematic analysis needs to give more attention to the problem of designing program structures to maximize

13. *Report of the National Advisory Commission on Civil Disorders,* p. 230.

fundings, and agencies will have to put together comprehensive packages of related programs to meet priority needs.

From the preceding discussion and from the analysis presented in the Appendix, in which the nature of program, appropriations, and obligations for fiscal 1969 are detailed, we can derive the following observations: there appears to be a great deal of cross-over in effort; in other words, many projects with similar scope and objectives are being administered independently of each other. Also, most programs affect either selected population groups or selected geographic areas, or sometimes both. From these observations we can draw the following conclusions: (1) Many programs are relatively new and are still developing or in some cases changing their program strategy and/or policy focus. This makes assessing their effectiveness difficult, if not impossible. Has the program reached its "target population"? What measure of "influences" has it exerted to guide future agency policy? Answers to these questions become seemingly impossible to quantify. (2) An urban development focus is frequently ignored or slighted in "urban" programs because so many of them are directed to only a segment of the population. (3) The need for a national urban development policy is self-evident.

National Urban Development Policy

In his State of the Union address, President Nixon called on Congress to join with him in developing "a national policy" which would channel the 100 million Americans who will be added to our population by the end of the century away from our large, congested metropolitan agglomerations towards alternative locations. The resident suggested a national policy "with the clear objective of aiding a balanced growth."[14] At the heart of this proposal is the formulation of a policy for urban centers relating to the migration of population and to economic development.

The limitations on a national policy can be drawn as broadly or as narrowly as desired. It is conceivable that aspects of government policy that touch on social, economic, cultural, political, and environmental phases of national life be included. A national policy should consider these component strategies: central city–ghetto economic development; ghetto dispersal; growth center strategy; and new towns.

Economic development programs should be directed to bringing new jobs to the central city and fostering minority entrepreneurship. The federal government should try to reverse the trend of decentralization of employment by offering location subsidies to firms which locate in the central city. Program priorities might include, among others: a *wage subsidy* on a per

14. Richard Nixon, *Public Papers of the Presidents of the United States* (Washington, D.C.: Government Printing Office, 1971), p. 14.

worker basis to enable firms to hire the disadvantaged at profitable rates during an initial work and training period; a lease *guarantee* program to attract business in the city; *loan guarantees* to encourage private lenders to undertake loans to firms to locate in the central city; *interest cost subsidies* to reduce the interest costs incurred in private financing of plants in central cities; *tax credits* to give tax rebates to those firms that locate in central cities; *procurement preferences* to give preference in federal procurement to firms that locate in central cities, *land assembly and development* to allow the federal government in conjunction with local governments to assemble and develop industrial sites and industrial parks in central cities. These measures should be augmented by the implementation of a computerized nationwide job information service with priority of location given to large urban centers.

In addition, the federal government should provide managerial and entrepreneurial training and ease of capital accessibility through such programs as lease and loan guarantees and interest rate subsidies to foster minority ownership. An economic development program should aim at strengthening already existing services in city locations and at providing more equitable, abundant and cheaper services.

Programs to provide commuter transportation services from the central city to suburban job opportunities might be expanded. Capital grants to or subsidization of these services offered by public or private rail or bus companies and payments to individual employers who run bus systems for their own employees are some possibilities.

The objective in ghetto dispersal would be to assimilate the residents of the central city ghetto into the overall metropolitan area on a more or less random basis. Emphasis would be placed upon the removal of barriers to the social and economic integration of the poor within the metropolitan area. This strategy would promote true freedom of choice in terms of individual rights and a spatial mixture of races. A major ingredient for accomplishing the objectives is housing; i.e., to reorient federal housing programs to place more emphasis on low- and moderate-income housing outside poverty areas. HUD's "Operation Breakthrough" is directed to this strategy.

Perhaps the most efficient use of public funds for urban development programs might be to encourage the growth of medium-sized urban centers, or growth centers, especially those that have already given real evidence of possessing growth and have strong ties to their surrounding regions. A growth center should be a place that maximizes the possibility of a person's finding employment and that maximizes the potential income that he could receive. Only those cities that could be expected to benefit a significant number of migrants by providing new jobs should be eligible as federally assisted growth centers. Such a strategy would *not* reinforce existing migration patterns that represent movement from rural areas to the large central city ghettos. Niles Hanson notes that both public locational preferences and efficient city sizes suggest that a growth center strategy should build on growing cities in the 250,000–750,000 population range, though somewhat wider limits should be considered for the sake of flexibility.[15]

If the growth center is to serve as a "migration alternative" to the large central city, then what measures should be undertaken to implement this strategy? The following measures may be considered: (1) federal financial incentives such as tax credits, business development loans, or even direct payment arrangements for business and industrial location; (2) federal investment assistance in amenities or in more directly productive infrastructure; (3) placement of federal procurement contracts and constructions projects; (4) expanded manpower and human resource development programs, with expanded comprehensive relocation assistance; (5) availability of a wide range of housing types at varying costs, including low-income housing. Although no definitive growth center strategy has as yet been worked out within the context of a national urbanization policy, the agencies that have been created to implement the programs have utilized the growth-center concept in their operations. These agencies are the Appalachian Regional Development Administration and the Economic Development Administration.

I have several comments on a new towns strategy. The National Committee on Urban Growth Policy has recommended that to help accommodate our expected population growth we construct new towns and new cities for 20 million people.[16] This proposal, however, would affect only a small part of our population and even a smaller part of housing production. Only 7 percent of the expected 300 million population would reside in these new settlements, and 80 percent of the predicted growth would occur in existing urban places. If replacement of one-third of the existing dwellings is taken into account, almost 90 percent of new housing would be produced in existing urban areas.

New towns and even new cities would of necessity be smaller, at least in the beginning, and the pattern of migration, especially for blacks, is to move away from smaller urban places to bigger ones. If we are to judge by existing cities of comparable size, quickly developed towns would be a poor magnet for migrants. Furthermore, most new town proposals are geared to relocating people within metropolitan areas, and their costs are such that they have

15. *Growth Center Policy in the United States*, Discussion Paper no. 4, (Center for Economic Development, the University of Texas at Austin, February 1970).

16. Cited by William Alonso, "What Are New Towns For?" Department of City and Regional Planning, University of California, Berkeley, Working Paper no. 108, October 1969. See also, National Committee on Urban Growth Policy, "Key National Leaders Recommend Large Program of New Cities for U.S." (Washington, D.C.: Urban America, new release dated May 25, 1969.)

little relevance to people in the income groups of those of most migrants from rural to urban areas.

Arguments favoring new towns have force if they are based on the development of sociotechnical improvements which could be applied to existing cities. To be useful, a new towns program would have to be replicable elsewhere.

An argument that appears reasonable is that urban physical development is hampered by a number of institutional circumstances, including local zoning, subdivision and building ordinances, and practices of the building craft unions. New towns could serve as laboratories for urban development and the concepts and modes of relevant legal regulations. It is conceivable that considerable reduction in cost could be achieved within present technology if intelligent and well-financed management and industrially organized labor were free to do their best. Even more might be achieved if there were technological advances.

Let me conclude by saying that a distinction should be made between a new towns strategy which aims at housing a substantial portion of the population and a policy which uses new towns to test innovations. More promising than a new town program would be a program to encourage growth in those smaller urban areas where there has been a history of viable economic development.

Information and Reference Sources

Using the information and records emerging from the operation of federal programs on urban development requires a familiarity with specific program operation generally not available to the community. Broad-gauged appraisals, reports, and evaluations of program operations are often prepared under the aegis of the administering agency. These reports most often include information concerning the activity levels, expenditure patterns, and general accomplishments of the specific operating program.

Increasing numbers of agencies have access to computerized information systems which store information concerning program operations which may be retrieved in a wide variety of formats. Such systems have promoted a greater centralization of information about program operations in local areas. As is always true of such systems, the information retrieved reflects the nature and quality of the original input. Nevertheless, the availability of more rapid retrieval does make it possible for the nonagency inquirer to seek and receive more extensive information than was possible in an earlier era of hand tabulation.

Perhaps more pertinent than the question of data availability is data use. Use of data for federal program application must, of course, be tailored to the requirements of that program. However, the use of data for research geared to the development of urban strategies depends on the creative idea, the technical expertise, and the availability of information resources from social, economic, and political data collection, as much as it does on the data recorded for federal program application and acceptance forms. The latter are most often the product of a research effort, and in my view dissemination of such research findings is the basis for the public discussion of improvements in the nation's urban environment.

The sources cited will be useful to researchers, planners, program developers, and other officials interested in federal programs to assist urban development. The citations are selective rather than exhaustive and include federal catalogs and handbooks; related publications by organizations of public officials; related research programs funded by the Economic Development Administration, Office of Economic Research; and other sources.

Federal Catalogs and Handbooks

1.   U.S., Congress, Senate. Committee on Government Operations. Subcommittee on Intergovernmental Relations. *Catalog of Federal Aids to State and Local Governments*. Prepared by the Legislative Reference Service of the Library of Congress. Washington, D.C., 1964. 154 pp.

2.   U.S., Congress. House of Representatives. *1969 Listing of Operating Federal Assistance Programs Compiled During the Roth Study*. Prepared by the Staff of Representative William V. Roth, Jr., 91st Congress, 1st Session, H. R. Document No. 91-177. Washington: Government Printing Office, 1969. 1,132 pp.

3.   U.S., Congress, Joint Economic Committee. *Federal Programs for the Development of Human Resources*. Washington, D.C., 1966.

4.   U.S. Department of Commerce. Economic Development Administration. *Handbook of Federal Aids to Communities*. Washington, 1966, 112 pp.

5.   U.S. Department of Commerce. Economic Development Administration. *EDA Handbook*. Washington, 1968.

6.   U.S. Department of Commerce. Office of Minority Business Enterprise. *Special Catalog of Federal Assistance Programs for Minority Business Enterprise*. Washington, September 1969, 141 pp.

7.   U.S., Department of Health, Education, and Welfare. Office of Program Analysis. *Grants-in-Aid and Other Financial Assistance Programs Administered by the Department of Health, Education, and Welfare*. Washington, D.C., 1967. 392 pp.

8.   U.S., Office of Economic Opportunity. *Catalog of Federal Domestic Assistance: A Description of the Federal Government's Domestic Programs to Assist the American People in Furthering Their Social and Economic Progress*. Washington, D.C., 1969. 610 pp.

Related Publications by Organizations of Public Officials

1. Advisory Commission on Intergovernmental Relations. *Impact of Federal Urban Development Programs on Local Government Organization and Planning.* Report 14-20. January 1964. 198 pp.

2. Advisory Commission on Intergovernmental Relations. *Intergovernmental Relations in the Poverty Program.* Report 14-29. Washington, D.C.: Government Printing Office, April 1966. 278 pp.

3. Advisory Commission on Intergovernmental Relations. *Metropolitan Social and Economic Disparities: Implications for Intergovernmental Relations in Central Cities and Suburbs.* Report A-25. Washington, D.C.: Government Printing Office, January 1965. 253 pp.

4. Advisory Commission on Intergovernmental Relations. *Urban America and the Federal System.* Report M-47. Washington, D.C.: Government Printing Office, October 1969. 140 pp.

5. Advisory Commission on Intergovernmental Relations. *Urban and Rural America: Policies for Future Growth.* Report A-32. Washington, D.C.: Government Printing Office, April 1968. 186 pp.

6. National Advisory Commission on Civil Disorders. *Report of the National Advisory Commission on Civil Disorders.* Washington, D.C.: Government Printing Office, March 1968. 425 pp.

7. National Commission on Urban Problems. *Building the American City.* Report of the National Commission on Urban Problems to the Congress and to the President of the United States. House Document 91-34. Washington, D.C.: Government Printing Office, 1969. pp. xi, 504.

8. National League of Cities. *Federal Aids to Local Governments.* Washington, D.C., 1966. 200 pp.

9. Report by the President's National Advisory Commission on Rural Poverty. *The People Left Behind.* Washington, D.C.: Government Printing Office, September 1969. 160 pp.

Related Research Programs Funded by the Economic Development Administration, Office of Economic Research

1. Harvard University. *Program on Regional and Urban Economics.* John F. Kain, Director.

2. Massachusetts Institute of Technology, Laboratory for Environmental Studies. *Dimensions of the Urban Problem and a National Policy for Urban Development.* Lloyd Rodwin, Director.

3. University of California, Berkeley. Center for Planning and Development Research. William Alonso, Director.

4. University of Chicago, Center for Urban Studies. *Research and Training Program in Regional Development Policy and Programming.* Jack Meltzer, Director.

5. University of Kentucky. *Program on the Role of Growth Centers in Regional Economic Development.* Alan R. Winger, Director.

6. University of Minnesota. *The Experimental City.* Walter Vivrett, Director.

7. University of Texas. *Role of Growth Centers in Regional Development Policy.* Niles Hansen, Director.

Other Sources

1. Hodge, Patricia L., and Philip M. Hauser. *The Challenge of America's Metropolitan Population: 1960 to 1985.* Prepared for the National Commission on Urban Problems. Praeger Special Studies in U.S. Economic and Social Development. Praeger, 1968.

2. Meyer, John R., John F. Kain, and Martin Wohl. *The Urban Transportation Problem.* Cambridge: Harvard University Press, 1965.

3. Perloff, Harver S., and Lowden Wingo, Jr. *Issues in Urban Economics.* Baltimore: Johns Hopkins Press, 1965.

4. Operations Research, Inc. *Feasibility Analysis of a Public Investment Data System.* Vols. 1 and 2 and appendixes. Silver Spring, Maryland, May 1967.

5. Schultze, Charles L., *The Politics and Economics of Public Spending.* Washington, D.C.: Brookings Institution, 1969.

6. Sundquist, James L., and David W. Davis, *Making Federalism Work.* Washington, D.C.: Brookings Institution, 1969.

7. Systemetrics: Division of Real Estate Research Corporation. *A Framework for Federal Policies and Programs concerning Urban Problems.* Washington, D.C., January 1969.

8. Department of Housing and Urban Development. *Urban and Regional Information Systems: Support for Planning in Metropolitan Areas.* Washington, D.C., 1968.

9. University of Illinois, Bureau of Community Planning. *Quarterly Digest of Urban and Regional Research.* Urbana, Ill.: University of Illinois Press.

10. Wilson, James Q., ed. *The Metropolitan Enigma.* Cambridge: Harvard University Press, 1968.

APPENDIX: SELECTED FEDERAL PROGRAMS DIRECTED TO URBAN DEVELOPMENT

Program Category	Authorizing Statute	Fiscal Year 1969 Appropriations Millions $	Fiscal Year 1969 Obligations Incurred Millions $	Nature of Program
1. Planning and Supportive Research				
Economic Development District Planning Assistance Grants (Department of Commerce, Economic Development Administration)	Title III(b) and Title IV (part B), Public Law 89-136	4.1	4.1	Objectives are to reduce unemployment and underemployment by supporting effective economic planning and action institutions at the multicounty level. This program provides technical assistance for the evaluation of the needs of the area. It also provides grants for resource development.
Urban Planning Research and Demonstration Program (Department of Housing and Urban Development)	Section 701(b), Housing Act of 1954	2.0	1.5 (5/31/69)	Objectives of the program are to develop and improve methods and techniques for comprehensive planning, to advance the purpose of comprehensive planning assistance program, and to assist in the conduct of research related to needed revisions of state statutes which create, govern, or control local governments or local governmental operations.
Comprehensive Planning Assistance—Grants	Section 701, Housing Act of 1954	43.8	43.8	The program provides federal grants to supplement state and local funds for assistance in community, regional, and statewide comprehensive planning.
General Research and Technology	12 U.S.C. 1701d-3; 1791e; 1701f; 79 Stat. 668; 80 Stat. 1286–1287	11.0	11.0	Research and development on urban development and housing problems to include the conduct of research and studies to test and demonstrate new and improved techniques and methods of applying advances in technology to housing construction, rehabilitation, maintenance and urban development activities: to encourage and promote the acceptance and application of new and improved techniques and methods of constructing, rehabilitating, and maintaining housing and the application of advances in technology to urban development activities, by all segments of the housing industry, communities, industries engaged in urban development ac-

Program	Authority			Description
Planning Grants (HUD)	Cities and Metropolitan Development Act of 1966			...financial and technical assistance to enable cities to plan, develop, and carry out comprehensive five-year local programs in selected areas, and to encourage new and imaginative proposals.
Highway Planning and Research Program (Department of Transportation)	23 U.S.C. 307(c)	69.0	72.0 (estimated)	This is a federal aid program designed to assist state highway departments in: (1) engineering and economic surveys and investigations; (2) planning of future highway programs and the financing thereof; (3) studies of the economy, safety, and convenience of highway usage and the desirable regulation and equitable taxation thereof; and (4) research and development necessary in the connection with the planning, design, construction, and maintenance of highways and highway systems and the regulation and taxation of their use.
Local Area Planning Grant Program (Department of Commerce, Economic Development Administration)	P.L. 89-136	0.64	0.64	Grants are made to assist local development groups to plan, staff, and implement economic development programs.
High-Speed Ground Transportation Research and Development (Department of Transportation)	Title I, P.L. 80-220	13.0	24.2	The objectives of the program are (1) to advance the technology of ground transportation, including railroads as well as more advanced systems; (2) to conduct research and development to make possible the design and demonstration of advanced ground transportation equipment, systems, and services; and (3) to develop cost and performance data on potential systems.
Economic Research Program (Department of Commerce, Economic Development Administration)	Title III, P.L. 89-136	3.0	3.0	The objective, as set forth in title III of the act, is to "establish and conduct a continuing program of study, training and research to (A) assist in determining the causes of unemployment, underemployment, underdevelopment and chronic depression in the various areas and regions of the Nation, (B) assist in the formulation and implementation of National, State, and local programs which

SOURCE: "1969 Listing of Operating Federal Assistance Programs Compiled during the Roth Study," by the staff of Congressman William V. Roth, Jr., 91st Cong., 1st sess., H. Doc. 91-177, 1,132 pp.

Program Category	Authorizing Statute	Fiscal Year 1969 Appropriations Millions $	Fiscal Year 1969 Obligations Incurred Millions $	Nature of Program
				will raise income levels and otherwise produces solutions to the problems resulting from these conditions, and (C) assist in providing the personnel needed to conduct such program."
Grants for Urban Mass Transportation—Technical Studies	P.L. 88-365—Section 9, Urban Mass Transportation Act of 1964	5.0	5.0	This grant program helps communities to undertake technical studies relating to management, operations, capital requirements, and economic feasibility; preparation of engineering and architectural surveys, plans, and specifications; and similar studies in preparation for the construction, acquisition, or improved operation of mass transportation systems.
Research and Demonstration Program—within Community Action Program (Office of Economic Opportunity)	Economic Opportunity Act of 1964, as amended	30.0	25.0 (estimated)	The research and demonstration program is designed to provide new knowledge and methods to assist and guide communities and community action programs so that they can, with the limited resources available to them, realize their full potential in the War on Poverty.
Community Development Training—Grants (HUD)	Title VIII, Housing Act of 1964	3.0	(None as of 6/26/69)	This project is designed to assist states in developing a continuing training program for state and local employees, for employees of public agencies with a community development responsibility, and for persons in training to be employees of state and local governments or public agencies. The objective of the program is to aid states and localities in coping with community development problems engendered by rapid urban growth.
Public Works Planning — Advances (HUD)	Section 702, Housing Act of 1954	7.5	7.5	This program provides assistance to states and their political subdivisions and to non-federal public agencies to assist them in planning essential public works and community facilities, except public housing to be constructed within a reasonable period. The planning advances are repaid to the federal government when construction begins.

Program	Authorizing legislation			Description
Community Renewal Program (HUD)	Title I, Housing Act of 1949	8.2 (funded by Urban Renewal appropriations)	8.2	The community renewal program is a method for assessing in broad terms the community's overall needs for renewal and developing a staged program for action, commensurate with the resources available to the community, to meet those needs.
2. Land Development; Urban Renewal; Maintenance				
Renewal Assistance Administration—Nonresidential Rehabilitation Loan (HUD)	Section 312, P.L. 88-560; SBA-HUD agreement dated March 20, 1967, and supplement no. 1 to agreement dated June 20, 1967	1.9	1.9	RAA loans are made to rehabilitate an entire property. Rehabilitation of the entire property is considered as one undertaking. Therefore, there may be one or many applicants who are owners of or tenants in the property to be rehabilitated, each of whom may need work done to bring the entire property into compliance with the applicable code requirements and the requirements and objectives of the Urban Renewal Plan.
Public Facility Loan (HUD)	Title II, Housing Amendment of 1955	40.0	40.0	This program provides long-term loans for the construction of all types of public works, other than school facilities, when such credit is not otherwise available on reasonable terms.
Demolition Grant Program (HUD)	Section 116, Housing Act of 1949	8.8	8.8	The demolition grant program provides technical assistance and grants to finance up to two-thirds of the cost of demolishing structures which state or local law determines to be structurally unsound. The locality must assure that displaced persons are relocated into decent, safe, and sanitary dwellings within their means. Demolition must be on a planned neighborhood basis.
Advance Acquisition of Land Grants (HUD)	Section 704, HUD Act of 1965	3.6	1.8	In order to encourage and assist in the propitious acquisition of land planned for future use for public purposes, the secretary is authorized to make grants to states and local public bodies and agencies to aid in financing the acquisition of a fee-simple title or other interest in such land.

Program Category	Authorizing Statute	Fiscal Year 1969 Appropriations Millions $	Fiscal Year 1969 Obligations Incurred Millions $	Nature of Program
Public Works and Economic Development Facilities (Department of Commerce, Economic Development Administration)	P.L. 89-136, as amended	180.0	169.3	The object of this project is to provide federal financial assistance for public works and economic development facilities.
Basic Water and Sewer Facilities (HUD)	Section 702, HUD Act of 1965	165.0	149.3	This program assists communities in the construction of adequate basic water and sewer facilities needed to promote efficient and orderly growth and development consistent with areawide comprehensive planning.
Interim Assistance for Blighted Areas—Grants (HUD)	Section 118, Housing Act of 1949	6.1	6.1	The purpose of these grants is to alleviate harmful conditions in slum and blighted areas. Generally, these are areas planned for urban renewal in the near future but in which some immediate public action is needed until permanent action can be taken.
Neighborhood Facilities Grants (HUD)	HUD Act of 1965	35.0	35.0	The objective of the program is to provide multipurpose neighborhood centers that offer programs of health, recreation, social, and similar community services. Priorities must be given to projects benefiting primarily persons of low incomes.
Neighborhood Development Program (HUD)	HUD Act of 1968	100.1	100.1	This program provides federal financial and technical assistance to communities on the basis of an annual increment for a renewal program which can cover activities in several contiguous or noncontiguous areas. All activities undertaken in the urban renewal program may be performed under this program.

3. Financial Aids

Program Category	Authorizing Statute	Fiscal Year 1969 Appropriations Millions $	Fiscal Year 1969 Obligations Incurred Millions $	Nature of Program
Lease Guarantee Program (Small Business Administration)	Title IV, Small Business Investment Act of 1958, and amendments of 1967 (P.L. 90-104)	None (A revolving fund of $5.0 million has been established and is self-sustaining.)	None (197 lease guarantee commitments have been established as of 6/30/69 for which maximum contingent liability	This program was established to enable small businesses to compete for business space on a more equal basis. It will supply the guarantee that the rent due the landlord by a small business tenant will be paid. This anticipates all types of small business—manufacturing, wholesaling, retailing, and servicing.

Program	Legislative authority	Appropriation	Amount	Description
Industrial Development Loans (Department of Commerce, Economic Development Administration)	Economic Development Administration Act of 1965 (P.L. 89-136)	50.0	44.4	Industrial development loans are provided to business firms expanding or establishing in economically depressed areas that have been designated by EDA as redevelopment areas or development districts.
Economic Opportunity Loans (SBA)	Title VI, Economic Opportunity Act of 1964	None[1]	47.0	The program is designed to provide financial and management assistance to low-income individuals or to those individuals who because of social or economic disadvantage have been denied the opportunity to acquire adequate business financing through normal lending channels on reasonable terms. It provides loans to expand or establish small businesses.
Guaranteed Business Loans (SBA)	Section 7(a), Small Business Act, as amended	None[1]	344.5	A loan is made by a lending institution under an agreement made with the Economic Development Administration. Upon default by borrower for 90 days (60 days, under the simplified blanket guaranty plan) of payment due on principal or interest, the bank may call upon SBA to purchase its guaranteed portion.
Participation Business Loans (SBA)	Section 7(a), Small Business Act, as amended	None[1]	138.1	A bank-serviced loan is made under an agreement executed by the bank and SBA; SBA will purchase from the bank, immediately upon disbursement by the bank, an agreed percentage of each disbursement. The loan is administered by the bank. SBA-serviced loans under this agreement: the bank will purchase from SBA, immediately upon disbursement, an agreed percentage of each disbursement made. The loan is administered by SBA.
Displaced Business Loans (SBA)	Section 7(b), Small Business Act, as amended	None[1]	28.0	Displaced business loans are made to assist small business concerns economically injured when displaced by, or located near any construction conducted by or with funds provided by the federal government.

[1] No appropriations sought in fiscal year 1969. The Participation Sales Act of 1966 authorizes Federal National Mortgage Association to sell "participation certificates" in pools of SBA loans, in order to provide needed funds for all SBA loan programs.

Program Category	Authorizing Statute	Fiscal Year 1969 Appropriations Millions $	Fiscal Year 1969 Obligations Incurred Millions $	Nature of Program
Pool Loans (SBA)	Section 7(a), Small Business Act, as amended	None[1]	None since 1964	A pool loan is made to a corporation formed and capitalized by a group of small business concerns with resources provided by them to obtain for the use of such concerns raw materials, equipment, inventories, or supplies or the benefit of research of development or the establishment of facilities for such purpose.
Direct Business Loans (SBA)	Section 7(a), Small Business Act, as amended	None[1]	13.9 (as of May 1969)	A loan made by the agency without bank participation or guarantee is a direct loan. Loans are made to help small manufacturers, wholesalers, retailers, service concerns, and other businesses get started, expand, grow, and prosper.
State Development Company Loans (SBA)	Section 501, Small Business Investment Act of 1958	5.0	None	The Small Business Administration is authorized to make loans to state development companies to implement the congressional policy to improve and stimuate the national economy in general and the small business segment by establishing a program to stimulate the flow of private equity capital and long-term loans for the sound financing of the operations, growth, expansion, and modernization of small business concerns.
Small Business Investment Company Program—Debentures (SBA)	Small Business Investment Act of 1958 (P.L. 85-699)	None[1]	9.7	The program was undertaken to improve and stimulate the national economy in general, and the small business segment in particular, by establishing a program to stimulate and supplement the flow of private equity capital and long-term loan funds which small business concerns need for the sound financing of their business operations and for their growth, expansion, and modernization and which are not available in adequate supply.
Local Development Company Loans (SBA and Commerce Department, Economic Devel-opment Administration)	Title V, Section 502, Small Business Investment Act of 1958	47.0	43.8	The purpose of this program is to improve and stimulate the national economy in general, and the small business segment in par-ticular, by establishing a program to stimu-

...and the flow of private equity capital and long-term loans for the sound financing of the operation, growth, expansion, and modernization of small business concerns.

4. Manpower

Program	Authority			Description
Experimental and Demonstration Program (Department of Labor, Manpower Administration)	Manpower Development and Training Act of 1962, as amended	15.0	15.0	The experimental and demonstration program seeks to develop, through actual project operation, new ideas and improved techniques and to demonstrate the effectiveness of specialized methods in meeting the manpower, employment, and training problems of particularly disadvantaged worker groups.
Labor Mobility Demonstration Projects (Department of Labor, Manpower Administration)	Manpower Development and Training Act of 1962, as amended	None	None (FY 1968: $4.4 million)	The objectives of the mobility projects are to explore the problems and potentials of financial, orientation, and related relocation aid to unemployed persons who cannot expect to find employment in their home area. The workers are relocated to specific jobs in areas of labor shortage.
Manpower Research Grants (Department of Labor, Manpower Administration)	Manpower Development and Training Act of 1962, as amended	1.2	1.2	Grants are made to public and private non-profit academic institutions and research organizations to broaden and strengthen national manpower research and operating program capability and to provide information needed for developing recommendations for policy and programs aimed at achieving the fullest development, utilization, and adjustment of the nation's manpower.
Manpower Development and Training	Manpower Development and Training Act of 1962, as amended	240.0	240.0	Occupational training, basic education, counseling, and supportive services are provided to unemployed and underemployed persons who cannot secure appropriate full-time employment without training. Training may also be provided for inmates of correctional institutions and residents of redevelopment areas as designated by the secretary of commerce.
Institutional Training (Department of Labor, Training and Employment Service, and Department of Health, Education, and Welfare, Office of Education)		(186.0)	(186.0)	

1 No appropriations sought in fiscal year 1969. The Participation Sales Act of 1966 authorizes Federal National Mortgage Association to sell "participation certificates" in pools of SBA loans, in order to provide needed funds for all SBA loan programs.

Program Category	Authorizing Statute	Fiscal Year 1969 Appropriations Millions $	Fiscal Year 1969 Obligations Incurred Millions $	Nature of Program
On-the-Job Training (Department of Labor, Manpower Administration)		(54.0)	(54.0)	
Manpower Research Contracts (Department of Labor, Manpower Administration)	Manpower Development and Training Act of 1962, as amended	4.5	4.5	Through contracts with academic institutions, state and local government organizations, and other organizations and individuals from all the social science disciplines with research capabilities in the manpower area, financial support is provided for studies of national manpower problems which will supply information needed for developing recommendations for policy and programs aimed at achieving the fullest development and utilization of the nation's manpower.
Special Impact Program (OEO)	Economic Opportunity Act of 1964 (P.L. 88-452), as amended P.L. 90-222	70.0	65.5 (estimated)	The purpose of this part is to establish special programs which (1) are directed to the solution of the critical problems existing in particular communities or neighborhoods (defined without regard to political or other subdivisions or boundaries) within those urban areas having especially large concentrations of low-income persons, and within those rural areas having substantial out-migration to eligible urban areas, and (2) are of sufficient size and scope to have an appreciable impact in such communities and neighborhoods in arresting tendencies toward dependency, chronic unemployment, and rising community tensions.
5. Technical Assistance and Services				
Technical Assistance (To Support Redevelopment Activities) (Department of Commerce, Economic and Development Administration)	Public Works and Economic Development Act of 1965 (P.L. 89-136)	10.3	10.3	This program provides technical assistance to help eligible areas evaluate their needs and to develop their potential for economic growth.

Program (Agency)	Legislation			Description
State Program Grants (Department of Commerce, State Technical Services)	Act of 1965 (P.L. 89-182)		(estimated)	port, not to exceed one-half the total cost, for the conduct of approved state technical services programs.
Special Program Grants (Department of Commerce, State Technical Services)	State Technical Services Act of 1965 (P.L. 89-182)	None	None	The Special Programs Division supports technical services programs that have broad regional or national significance or that employ new techniques or methods not included in state programs.
State Technical Services Program—Planning Grants (Department of Commerce, State Technical Services)	State Technical Services Act of 1965 (P.L. 89-182)	None (not authorized beyond FY 1968)	None	The objective of the program is to encourage the more effective application of science and technology in business, commerce, and industry. Planning grants are made for the preparation or revision of a state's technical services, workshops, seminars, training programs, and so forth.

6. Transportation Planning and Development

Program (Agency)	Legislation			Description
Urban Mass Transportation Research Development and Demonstration (Department of Transportation, Urban Mass Transportation Administration)	Urban Mass Transportation Act of 1964, as amended (P.L. 88-365)	18.5	18.5	The administration is authorized to undertake research, development, and demonstration projects in all phases of urban mass transportation for the purpose of assisting in the reduction or urban transportation needs, the improvement of mass transportation service, or the meeting of total urban transportation needs at minimum cost. The projects include the development, testing, and demonstration of new facilities, equipment, techniques, and methods.
Federal Aid Airport Program (Department of Transportation, Federal Aviation Administration)	Federal Airport Act of 1964	70.0	88.5 (estimated)	The airport program makes grants to public agencies for airport development to assist in bringing about, in conformity with the national airport plan, the establishment of a nationwide system of public airports adequate to meet the present and future needs of civil aviation.
Urban Mass Transportation Capital Grants and Loans (Department of Transportation, Urban Mass Transportation Administration)	Urban Mass Transportation Act of 1964, Sections 3–5, (P.L. 88-365)	148.3	148.3 (estimated)	The objective of the program is through capital improvement grants or loans (but not both for the same project), to provide financial assistance to urban communities for improving and upgrading their mass transportation facilities and equipment.

Federal Assistance to Cities, 1900–1930

JOSEPH B. HOWERTON

The title of this portion of the conference has puzzled me. The word impact —it is one of those dramatic words, and I have always associated it with destructive force, shock, cries of anguish—in fact, when it is used I always expect sound effects. Now the effect of some federal activities on cities can undoubtedly be regarded in this way, and maybe particularly some that have focused on this city—although Washington *is* atypical. I wondered if my task of describing records to whet the reader's appetite for research would involve looking for grisly relics of urban victims of federal power. But my preference is for constructive activities, and I have chosen to think of the use of the word in this context as a gimmick and that I can interpret it in a wider sense.

Papers that describe some federal activities that affect urban areas have been prepared by members of the staff of the National Archives. Those papers that are particularly appropriate for this panel are Ed Hill's on public works in Sacramento; Bob Kvasnicka's on federal relief agencies and Detroit; and Bill Sherman's on the economic development of San Francisco.[1]

At this juncture I want to call attention to some records regarding services, mostly informal, that federal agencies were performing for cities during the period from roughly 1900 to 1930. My investigation was prompted by a handbook of federal services available to cities, published in 1931 by

This paper was shortened by the omission of much detailed administrative history data, records description, and illustrative material. I have, therefore, cited in these footnotes pertinent reference materials as well as sources of those specific items of information mentioned in the text.

1. Preliminary drafts prepared for the Conference on the National Archives and Urban Research, June 1970, include: "Records in the National Archives Relating to Public Works in the City of Sacramento," by Edward E. Hill; "City in Crisis: The Impact of Depression on Detroit, Michigan, as Reflected in Records of the Federal Relief Agencies," by Robert M. Kvasnicka; and "Selected Records of the Departments of the Treasury and Commerce Relating to the Economic Development of San Francisco, 1847–1967," by William F. Sherman. Also relevant is the paper, "Military Development and Urban Growth in the San Francisco Bay Area prior to World War II," prepared for the conference by William H. Cunliffe.

the Municipal Administrative Service and prepared by Paul V. Betters of the Brookings Institution's Institute for Government Research.[2] This compilation was based on a thorough survey of federal agencies and it lists somewhere between 100 and 150 services that could be requested by city governments. More than forty agencies were named. The services described took the form of various kinds of assistance and aid that the federal agencies could perform and cooperative activities of federal and city officials and professionals in administrative and technical areas. These ranged from supplying publications and testing materials to assistance in the prevention and suppression of epidemics and the sale of water and electricity. Programs affecting cities that resulted from federal grants-in-aid and subsidies to states and activities that have always been recognized as the sole responsibility of the central government were specifically omitted from the compilation.

I was impressed by the number of participating agencies and the variety of services offered and decided to see if federal records show whether or not cities made any great use of these services. Accordingly, I examined records of several of the agencies named by Betters to locate documentation of some of the services that he described.

Please try to bear up under what follows here. Description of records is not the most stimulating type of writing. I know that from long experience, but I hope the reader will not grow very bored by this not too lengthy account of what I have found.

For the Public Health Service, Betters listed services under thirteen categories, such as research activities, sanitary surveys, assistance in epidemics, laboratory services, administrative assistance, and informational services.[3] In the records for the period 1897 to 1922, I found considerable quantities of material that documented cooperation with health authorities of a number of municipalities in combating and preventing diseases.[4] For example, the records show that Public Health Service professionals were assigned to help city health officers during epidemics of typhoid as early as 1906.[5] Con-

2. Paul V. Betters, *Federal Services to Municipal Governments*, Municipal Administration Service Publication no. 24 (New York, 1931). For more detailed information about the administrative histories and functions of many of the various agencies listed in this compilation, see also the individual "Service Monographs" of the Brookings Institution's Institute for Government Research, published during the 1920s. I cite those monographs for the agencies referred to in the text.

3. Ibid., pp. 70–79. See also Laurence F. Schmeckebier, *The Public Health Service: Its History, Activities, and Organization*, Brookings Institution, Institute for Government Research, Service Monographs of the United States Government, no. 10 (Baltimore: Johns Hopkins Press, 1923), pp. 103–4.

4. Records of the Public Health Service, Record Group 90, National Archives Building, Washington, D.C. (Hereafter records in the National Archives Building are indicated by the symbol NA.)

5. File 4141 in particular, General Classified File, 1897–1923, Record Group 90, NA.

currently, federal agents furnished assistance in locating and eliminating sources of water pollution, and in testing and evaluating various types of equipment designed for sewage disposal and water purification.[6] Public Health Service officials and city health officials cooperated in gathering and reporting data on vital reports as early as 1902.[7] For the years of World War I, there is, of course, a great deal of material on assistance rendered to cities during the flu epidemic,[8] which is a popular topic, but there are also quantities of records documenting cooperation with city authorities in the control of sanitary conditions and diseases around military establishments and war production plants in numerous urban areas.[9]

By the 1920s, relations between the Public Health Service and cities had apparently become so cordial that authorities of a city in Alabama turned to Washington as a matter of course for advice on getting rid of what they called "Water Dogs" that were infesting the city's water mains. (These turned out to be examples of a species of salamander—up to a foot long.)[10]

The Food and Drug Administration and its predecessors also worked closely with city health officials.[11] The general correspondence of the agency, which begins in 1919,[12] includes files relating specifically to cooperative work with city officials.[13] These show that the agency coordinated work with state and local officials in the determination of standards and the enforcement of laws relating to pure foods and drugs. The files document a policy decision by the agency as to whether or not its officials and agents should be allowed to serve on city boards of health. Apparently there were cases in which the federal officials had been invited to serve on the local boards because of the reputation of their positions with the federal government and their close working relationships with city authorities.

Files of the Bureau of Animal Industry for the period of 1895–1925 show that the agency furnished advice and assistance to city officials in drafting ordinances for the regulation of and in improving administrative procedures

6. Files 3450 and 126 in particular, ibid.

7. File 2451 in particular, ibid.

8. File 1622, ibid.

9. File 4017, ibid.

10. Boards of Health, Alabama, General Classified File, 1923–35, RG 90, NA. This segment of the file is arranged by names of states, and there is a separate section within each state file for materials that relate to municipal boards of health.

11. Betters, *Federal Services to Municipal Governments,* pp. 42–43. See also Gustavus A. Weber, *The Food, Drug, and Insecticide Administration: Its History, Activities, and Organization,* Brookings Institution, Institute for Government Research, Service Monographs of the United States Government, no. 50 (Baltimore: Johns Hopkins Press, 1928), pp. 22, 45.

12. In Records of the Food and Drug Administration, Record Group 88, NA.

13. File 660, Cooperation with State and Local Officials, ibid. The files are arranged in yearly segments.

for local meat inspection.[14] This bureau in 1906 had to decline the request of city officials in Buffalo and Cincinnati to have federal agents serve as city meat inspectors (although the bureau assured the city authorities of its desire to furnish aid and cooperation).[15] In 1909, Boston tried to have bureau agents inspect the city's out-of-state sources of milk.[16] In 1911, the bureau was developing plans for a model municipal abattoir.[17]

The files of the Bureau of Dairy Industry for the period 1922–30 show that this agency was furnishing advice and assistance to cities for their milk inspection systems similar to that furnished by the Bureau of Animal Industry for meat inspection.[18]

The general files of the Children's Bureau for the period 1912–20 include records documenting the bureau's extensive surveys of child life and welfare in individual cities, which were made with the cooperation of city authorities.[19] These records refer to surveys on the use of work certificates in Norwalk, Connecticut, in 1913;[20] recreational facilities in the District of Columbia in 1914;[21] child labor in Boston in 1915;[22] infant mortality, birth registration, housing, infant welfare work, hospitals, cost of living, boarding houses,

14. In File 111, Central Correspondence, 1913–1939, Records of the Bureau of Animal Industry, Record Group 17, NA. The general correspondence files of the bureau for the period 1895–1939 are in several chronological segments, each having sections containing materials relating to cooperation with city officials. For discussions of the functions of the bureau regarding city services, see Betters, *Federal Services to Municipal Governments*, pp. 38–39; and Fred Wilbur Powell, *The Bureau of Animal Industry: Its History, Activities, and Organization*, Brookings Institution, Institute for Government Research, Service Monographs of the United States Government, no. 41 (Baltimore: Johns Hopkins Press, 1927), pp. 34–37.

15. File 4459, Central Correspondence, 1895–1906, RG 17, NA.

16. File 530, Central Correspondence, 1907–13; ibid.

17. File 458, ibid.

18. Records of the Bureau of Dairy Industry, Record Group 52, NA. In the General Records of the Dairy Division, Bureau of Animal Industry, 1922–24, see especially Files 405 and 444. In the General Correspondence Files of the Bureau of Dairy Industry, 1925–39, see Files 130 through 139 and 470 through 479. For discussions of the functions of the Bureau of Dairy Industry pertaining to city services, see Betters, *Federal Services to Municipal Governments*, p. 41; and Jenks Cameron, *The Bureau of Dairy Industry: Its History, Activities, and Organization*, Brookings Institution, Institute for Government Research, Service Monographs of the United States Government, no. 55 (Baltimore: Johns Hopkins Press, 1929), p. 26.

19. Records of the Children's Bureau, Record Group 102, NA. The files are arranged in chronological segments covering, usually, about four years each. For discussions of the bureau's functions about services to cities, see Betters, *Federal Services to Municipal Governments*, pp. 67–68; and James A. Tobey, *The Children's Bureau: Its History, Activities, and Organization*, Brookings Institution, Institute for Government Research, Service Monographs of the United States Government, no. 21 (Baltimore: Johns Hopkins Press, 1925), especially pp. 3, 4, 15–17, 22–23.

20. File 6722, General Files, 1914–20, RG 102, NA.

21. File 5-5, ibid.

22. Files 6511, 6512, and 6-0-1-2, ibid.

and conditions under which Negroes lived in the city, for Baltimore, during the period 1913–16;[23] and infant mortality in Johnstown, Pennsylvania,[24] Montclair, New Jersey,[25] Manchester, New Hampshire,[26] Brockton, Massachusetts,[27] and Saginaw, Michigan.[28]

Detailed information, used to evaluate city educational programs, was obtained through school surveys of the Bureau of Education, which were conducted at the request and with the cooperation of city school authorities.[29] The records of the Office of Education contain files relating to surveys in about thirty cities.[30] In addition, files regarding surveys in three counties and fourteen states include some information about city school systems. The surveys are concentrated in the period 1911–26. Files for a survey of Buffalo's schools, which was conducted a little later, during the years 1928–32, are quite voluminous, comprising in excess of two cubic feet.

Files of field service reports, submitted by members of the staff of the Office of Education on assignments, record the names of cities visited by the staff members and the services they rendered (that is, if they delivered speeches, attended conferences, participated in studies, etc.). Also, the reports identify the local bodies or officials who requested the services.[31] These reports document a wide variety of informational, consultative, and technical services and the expert assistance rendered to cities by the Bureau of Education. And they show a close relationship existing between the bureau and city school authorities during the period under consideration.

In 1914, the secretary of labor inaugurated a service that was essentially an adult education program in English and citizenship for aliens who had applied for naturalization.[32] This became known as the "Americanization program." The plan called for close cooperation between the Bureau of Nat-

23. Files 11, 532 through 11, 548, ibid.
24. Files 11, 410 to 11, 420, ibid.
25. Files 11, 420 to 11, 430, ibid.
26. Files 11, 430 to 11, 440, ibid.
27. Files 11, 440 to 11, 450, ibid.
28. Files 11, 450 to 11, 460, ibid.
29. Betters, *Federal Services to Municipal Governments*, pp. 49–54. See also Darrell Hevenor Smith, *The Bureau of Education: Its History, Activities, and Organization*, Brookings Institution, Institute for Government Research, Service Monographs of the United States Government, no. 14 (Baltimore: Johns Hopkins Press, 1923), especially pp. 45 and 70–72 and "Educational Surveys," Bureau of Education Bulletin no. 11 (1928), pp. 19–41.
30. Files of the Office of the Commissioner of Education, ca. 1908–32, Records of the Office of Education, Record Group 12, NA.
31. Ibid.
32. Betters, *Federal Services to Municipal Governments*, p. 69. See also Darrell Hevenor Smith, *The Bureau of Naturalization: Its History, Activities, and Organization,* Brookings Institution, Institute for Government Research, Service Monographs of the United States Government, no. 43 (Baltimore: Johns Hopkins Press, 1926), especially pp. 11, 12, 28, 57.

uralization and the public schools. The records of the Immigration and Naturalization Service for the period of 1915–30 document the participation of literally hundreds of city school systems in this project.[33] There are separate files for individual cities which contain information about the establishment of the program and its continuing operation and progress and include statistical data and narrative accounts of the local participation.

The records of the Bureau of Public Roads and its predecessors include files relating to a program begun in the late 1890s, in which the agency donated the services of its engineers to supervise the construction of short stretches of road to demonstrate proper design and techniques in the use of materials and equipment.[34] These "Object Lesson Roads" projects were continued until about 1916, when direct federal aid to the states for road construction was begun. Although the supervising engineer worked most closely with state and county officials, the files are arranged under the names of the cities made accessible by road construction, and they document cooperation with city engineers and officials and contain information about streets of cities and towns.[35] For the benefit of those researchers who may be interested in data of this type, the files also contain the engineer's weekly reports, which show the organization of the labor force, types of materials and equipment used, and costs of labor and materials. Incidentally, the engineers frequently report the use of convict labor in the southern and western states, and, in one file for a project in Louisiana in 1909, the engineer reported the use of "lunatics."[36]

Files of the Bureau of Biological Survey for the period 1902–30 document the bureau's assistance to cities in rat control projects and in furnishing domestic wild animal specimens to municipal zoos and museums.[37]

33. Files relating to the Americanization Program, Records of the Immigration and Naturalization Service, Record Group 85, NA.

34. In Records of the Bureau of Public Roads, Record Group 30, NA. For discussions of the functions of the bureau in relation to this project and others that affect municipalities, see W. Stull Holt, *The Bureau of Public Roads: Its History, Activities, and Organization*, Brookings Institution, Institute for Government Research, Service Monographs of the United States Government, no. 26 (Baltimore: Johns Hopkins Press, 1923), especially pp. 8–9, 10–12; and Betters, *Federal Services to Municipal Governments,* p. 47.

35. General Correspondence, 1893–1912 (separate files under names of cities); and General Correspondence and Related Records, 1912–50 (File 420), RG 30, NA.

36. File 50, Alexandria, La., General Correspondence, 1893–1912, ibid.

37. In General Correspondence and Other Records of the Bureau of Biological Survey, 1890–1944, Records of the Fish and Wildlife Service, Record Group 22, NA. For data about rodent control, see files under the subject "Predatory Animal and Rodent Control," particularly under subsections, "cooperation" and "rats;" and for data about animal specimens furnished to zoos and museums, see files under subjects "Big Game" and "Alaska Game Laws." For discussions of the functions of the bureau's city services, see Betters, *Federal Services to Municipal Governments,* pp. 39–40; and Jenks Cameron, *The Bureau of Biological Survey: Its History, Activities, and Organi-*

Indexes to the labor case files of the United States Conciliation Service, 1913–30, contain references to the agency's services in mediating labor disputes involving such city employees as clerical workers and garbage collectors.[38]

Correspondence of the National Bureau of Standards documents tests of materials and substances performed for city agencies and the furnishing of specifications for various types of equipment.[39]

The subject file of the Geography Division of the Bureau of the Census contains correspondence with town and city authorities and chambers of commerce that deal with such matters as cooperative procedures for taking the census; defining enumeration districts and boundaries; furnishing information about methods used by the Census Bureau in arriving at data about various cities; and inclusion of cities in a study made of metropolitan areas for the 1930 census.[40] The schedules of the decennial censuses and other records of the Bureau of the Census, needless to say, contain a vast amount and variety of data about cities.

Throughout World War I, the Bureau of Markets and its predecessors operated programs offering services to cities in the marketing of agricultural produce. Appropriations for these services were discontinued by Congress after the war. The records of the Bureau of Markets contain a considerable quantity of material relating to these services, and information about municipal markets.[41] The most important of the bureau's services were offered

zation, Brookings Institution, Institute for Government Research, Service Monographs of the United States Government, no. 54 (Baltimore: Johns Hopkins Press, 1929), pp. 168, 179.

38. In Records of the Federal Mediation and Conciliation Service, Record Group 280, NA. For a discussion of the functions of the United States Conciliation Service, see Joshua Bernhardt, *The Division of Conciliation: Its History, Activities, and Organization,* Brookings Institution, Institute for Government Research, Service Monographs of the United States Government, no. 20 (Baltimore: Johns Hopkins Press, 1925).

39. In Records of the National Bureau of Standards, Record Group 167, NA. For discussions of the functions of the bureau relating to city services, see Betters, *Federal Services to Municipal Governments,* pp. 5–16; and Gustavus A. Weber, *The Bureau of Standards: Its History, Activities, and Organization,* Brookings Institution, Institute for Government Research, Service Monographs of the United States Government, no. 35 (Baltimore: Johns Hopkins Press, 1925), pp. 178, 180–83.

40. In Records of the Bureau of the Census, Record Group 29, NA. For discussions of the functions of the bureau services to cities, see Betters, *Federal Services to Municipal Governments,* pp. 32–34; and W. Stull Holt, *The Bureau of the Census: Its History, Activities, and Organization,* Brookings Institution, Institute for Government Research, Service Monographs of the United States Government, no. 53 (Washington, D.C.: Brookings Institution, 1929), pp. 69, 83, 133. See also U.S., National Archives and Records Service, *Records of the Bureau of the Census,* Preliminary Inventory no. 161, comps. Katherine H. Davidson and Charlotte M. Ashby (Washington, D.C., 1964). The subject files of the Geography Division, 1889–1950, are described under series 160 in the inventory.

41. In Records of the Bureau of Agricultural Economics, Record Group 83, NA.

through the operations of its "City Marketing and Distribution Project," which encouraged the development of municipally controlled public markets and supervised the operation of a city marketing reporting service.[42] During the period 1913–21, the files show that the agency studied commercial methods used in distributing and marketing food in urban areas to develop efficient and economical procedures; corresponded with city governments interested in creating municipal marketing systems; developed plans for model markets; and provided information, advice, and assistance to city officials. It cooperated with local markets in developing a reporting service in which data about kinds, amounts, and prices of produce brought to local markets were gathered and reported daily in the markets and in local newspapers.

The records of the Bureau of Agricultural Economics also include records relating to the operation of the Center Market in the District of Columbia.[43] This was probably the oldest and largest market in the city, its operation reputedly dating from 1802. It was taken over by the federal government in 1921, and the records reflect the operation of the Center Market by the Bureau of Agricultural Economics until about 1930 or 1931, when it was torn down to clear the site for the construction of the National Archives.

And so we find ourselves back where the records are, safe, secure, and waiting to be used.

It would be impossible for me to describe National Archives holdings of records relating to services offered by the agencies named in Betters's handbook in any reasonable length of time. I have not even reported all of the data I found in my short investigation. The time limitation made my research hasty and my examination of the records cursory. To find what I have described, I limited myself to skimming through finding aids prepared at the National Archives to locate and examine the most promising files. And, by the way, despite the complaining we get about our inventories and

The administrative history of the marketing functions of the Department of Agriculture are rather complicated. See U.S., National Archives and Records Service, *Records of the Bureau of Agricultural Economics*, Preliminary Inventory no. 104, comp. Vivian Wiser (Washington, D.C., 1958). See also idem, *Preliminary Inventory of the Records of the Agricultural Marketing Service (Record Group 136)*, Preliminary Inventory no. NC-118, comp. Virgil E. Baugh (Washington, D.C., 1965). For a discussion of the functions of the Bureau of Agricultural Economics pertaining to city services, see Betters, *Federal Services to Municipal Governments*, pp. 37–38.

42. Records Relating to the City Marketing and Distribution Project (series 11 in Preliminary Inventory no. 104), Record Group 83, NA; see also File 61, "City Marketing," in the Numerical General Correspondence File of the Bureau of Markets and Its Predecessors, 1912–22 (series 3 in Preliminary Inventory no. 104), Record Group 83, NA; and Office File of R. M. Beanfield, 1916–17 (series 8 in Preliminary Inventory no. 104), Record Group 83, NA. Beanfield was a structural engineer concerned with design of buildings and facilities of municipal markets.

43. Records Relating to the Operation of the Center Market, 1921–30 (series 30 in Preliminary Inventory no. 104), Record Group 83, NA.

finding aids, some of it recent, they are a great help if one takes a little time to get experience using them.

I have touched on documentation of a few of the services offered to cities by only a baker's dozen of the forty-odd agencies listed in the 1931 handbook. Documentation of some, of course, has undoubtedly disappeared in the forty years since the manual was published. Some had probably been lost by the time Betters compiled it. Despite this I am certain that more remains than what I have just accounted for. Of course, a researcher may have to really dig to find some of it. Then, too, since the manual was compiled in 1930 or 1931, very likely some services that had been furnished earlier had been dropped by the agencies and so were not mentioned in the survey. For example, Betters did not mention the program of "Object Lesson Roads" furnished by the Office of Public Roads.

These records I have described document an area that has been given little attention in detail by historians, as far as I can discover. The political scientist Daniel Elazar has developed a conceptualization of federal-city relationships during the period from 1900 to 1930, and I think the data I have seen tends to bear out his analysis in many, if not in all, respects.[44] Most accounts by historians of federal-city relations that I have seen recently give slight discussion to the subject of increasing contacts between federal agencies and city governments from the time of around the turn of the century up to the time of the depression; the cross-fertilization of bureaucracies; the use made by cities of the superior resources, facilities, and expertise of the national government; and the diplomatic imposition of federal standards. I have been unable to find any full historical treatment or evaluation of the effects of these relations on cities, or the effect of this type of activity and cooperation on federal-city relationships. Yet, as the evidence I have seen shows, the intergovernmental contacts were numerous. It may prove to be an interesting story, or, probably many interesting stories.

44. Daniel J. Elazar, "The Shaping of Intergovernmental Relations in the Twentieth Century," *Annals of the American Academy of Political and Social Science: Intergovernmental Relations in the United States* (May 1965). See also Daniel J. Elazar, "Urban Problems and the Federal Government: A Historical Inquiry," *Political Science Quarterly* 82 (December 1967), pp. 505–25.

Contributors

DONALD J. BOGUE

Dr. Bogue, a specialist in population and urban sociology, is a professor at the University of Chicago and director of the university's Community and Family Study Center. He has also been a consultant to the Bureau of the Census and the Budget and the Technical Assistance Administration of the United Nations. His published works include *The Structure of the Metropolitan Community* (1971), *Economic Areas of the United States* (1961), and *The Principles of Demography* (1969). Dr. Bogue served as chairman of the panel on population at the conference.

RICHARD OAKLEY DAVIES

Dr. Davies, director of the Center for Integrated Studies and professor of history at Northern Arizona University, has specialized in recent American history with some emphasis on social welfare, particularly housing. In addition to being the author of numerous articles in historical and sociological journals Dr. Davies has written *Housing Reform During the Truman Administration* (1966), and has been coeditor of *America's Recent Past* (1969).

GERALD L. DUSKIN

Mr. Duskin is a regional economist at the Economic Development Administration of the United States Department of Commerce. A former faculty member of Rutgers University, University College, he has served as a research specialist in that university's Bureau of Economic Research. He has been director of the Socio-Economic and Land Use Study of the New York Metropolitan Region, and an economist for several states. Mr. Duskin is the author of technical studies of the economic development of the New Jersey meadowlands and various EDA reports prepared for symposia on urban and rural development.

JEROME FINSTER

Mr. Finster, a long-time member of the National Archives staff, is chief of its Industrial and Social Branch, which specializes in records of federal agencies

159

operating in socioeconomic fields, particularly labor and transportation, but also housing, business, social welfare, and science.

HERBERT G. GUTMAN

Dr. Gutman, chairman, History Department, City University of New York, is a specialist on the working class and the transition of society to the industrial-urban era. His articles in journals and in books include "The Negro and the United Mine Workers" and "Social Status, Class, and Community Power in the Industrial City," in addition to the book, *The Invisible Fact: A Social History of the Black Family*.

GLEN E. HOLT

Dr. Holt, a specialist in transportation, is assistant professor of history at Washington University and assistant director of its Institute for Urban and Regional Studies. His published works include "Urban Mass Transit as Pathology and Problem Solver," in Kenneth T. Jackson and Stanley K. Schultz, eds., *American History: The Urban Perspective*; and *Mass Transit in St. Louis 1858–1884: A Case Study of an Urban Institution*. Dr. Holt is junior author for Harold M. Mayer and Richard C. Wade, *Chicago: Growth of a Metropolis*.

JOSEPH B. HOWERTON

Mr. Howerton, assistant chief of the National Archives Industrial and Social Branch, specializes in federal records pertaining to labor, business and industry, and social welfare. He has also dealt extensively with records of agencies operating in the technical and scientific fields and with naval records.

WILLIAM EDMUND LIND

Mr. Lind, a veteran member of the National Archives staff, is a specialist in genealogical records and archives administration. He serves the agency as a research consultant.

JEROME P. PICKARD

Dr. Pickard has been consultant for the Appalachian Regional Commission since July 1970. He was director of Program Analysis and Evaluation at the United States Department of Housing and Urban Development, 1967–70, director of research at the Urban Land Institute, 1960–67, and research director of the metropolitan Washington Board of Trade, 1954–59. In these and other positions he has had extensive experience in urban research and in economic and social analysis. Dr. Pickard has also served on the faculties of American University, the George Washington University, the University of Maryland, and the State University of New York. He is the author of *Metropolitanization of the United States* (1959), *Dimensions of Metropolitanism,* 2 vols. (1967–68), and *U.S. Metropolitan Growth and Expansion, 1970–2000* (1971).

LEONARD RAPPORT

Mr. Rapport, a veteran member of the National Archives, is now with the Records Appraisal Staff. He has been extensively involved with the records relating to transportation, labor, and social welfare. From 1958 to 1969 Mr. Rapport was associate editor of the Documentary History of the Ratification of the Federal Constitution and the First Ten Amendments, a project of the National Historical Publications Commission. From July 1970 to July 1971 he was on leave of absence from the Records Appraisal Division on a grant from the National Endowment for the Humanities, conducting a critical examination of the original manuscript notes kept by James Madison in the Federal Convention. His findings will be incorporated in a new edition, being prepared by Mr. Rapport, of Max Farrand's *Records of the Federal Convention of 1787.* Mr. Rapport is coauthor of *Rendezvous With Destiny* (1948; second edition, 1965), which is a history of the World War II 101st Airborne Division of the United States Army. He has also contributed chapters in several other published volumes and has contributed articles to the *Virginia Quarterly Review,* the *American Archivist,* and other journals.

HENRY B. SCHECHTER

Dr. Schechter has been senior specialist in housing, Congressional Research Service, Library of Congress, since October 1970. Previously, from 1966, he had been director, Office of Economic and Market Analysis, Department of Housing and Urban Development. In his present capacity he serves as a consultant to Congress in respect to housing, urban development, and related economic and financial matters. In addition to his service with other federal agencies, Dr. Schechter has represented the United States government on various groups concerned with housing, economic affairs, and urban development, in this country and abroad. He is the author of numerous published articles and papers on housing including its financial and marketing aspects.

ELIZABETH K. SCHOENECKER

Mrs. Schoenecker, a graduate of Marquette and Georgetown universities, has been with the Department of Housing and Urban Development since 1968. Since 1969 she has been an economist with the Office of Economic Analysis, working on matters dealing with national housing needs and production.

SAM BASS WARNER, JR.

Dr. Warner is William Edwards Huntington Professor of History and Social Science at Boston University. He has also been professor of history at the University of Michigan and is a well-known urban historian. He was formerly associated with the Joint Center for Urban Studies (of Harvard University and the Massachusetts Institute of Technology) and the Center for Urban and Regional Studies of Washington University. Professor Warner is the author of *Street-Car Suburbs: The Process of Growth in Boston, 1870–1900* (1969), *The Private City: Philadelphia in Three Periods of Its Growth* (1971), and *The Urban Wilderness: A History of the American City* (1972).

WILLIAM H. WILSON

Dr. Wilson is on the faculty of North Texas State University and was formerly on the faculties of the University of South Dakota and the University of Alaska. His research and publications have been concerned with urban history, particularly in Kansas City, and with Alaskan history. He is the author of *The City Beautiful Movement in Kansas City* (1964), and he is preparing works on the Alaska Railroad and works on urban United States in the period 1915–45.

Appendix:
National Archives Resource Papers

The following resource papers were distributed at the Conference on the National Archives and Urban Research. They are available upon request from the National Archives.

"Materials Relating to Urban Affairs in the National Archives and Audiovisual Branch"
THE STAFF OF THE AUDIOVISUAL BRANCH

"Military Development and Urban Growth in the San Francisco Bay Area prior to World War II"
WILLIAM H. CUNLIFFE

"Housing Records in the National Archives for Nashville and Atlanta"
KATHERINE H. DAVIDSON

"Cartographic Records in the National Archives of the United States Useful for Urban Studies"
RALPH E. EHRENBERG

"Records in the National Archives Relating to Public Works in the City of Sacramento"
EDWARD E. HILL

"Some Sources of Federal Documentation of Minority Groups in Chicago"
JOSEPH B. HOWERTON

"City in Crisis: The Impact of Depression on Detroit, Michigan, as Reflected in Records of the Federal Relief Agencies"
ROBERT M. KVASNICKA

"Urban Housing and Rental Data in the Records of the Rent Commission of the District of Columbia"
KATHRYN M. MURPHY

"Records in the National Archives Relating to Immigration to Boston"
CARMELITA S. RYAN

"Selected Records of the Departments of the Treasury and Commerce Relating to the Economic Development of San Francisco, 1847–1967"
WILLIAM F. SHERMAN
"Records in the National Archives Relating to Transportation in Chicago"
GEORGE S. ULIBARRI

Date Due

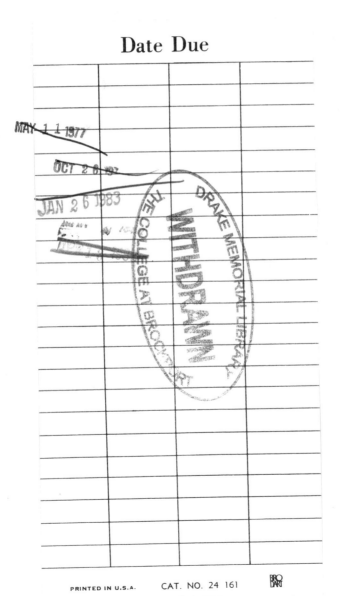

WARNER & HANNA'S

PLAN

of the City and Environs of

Baltimore;

Respectfully dedicated to the Mayor, City Council

& Citizens thereof, by the Proprietors, 1801.